What's wrong with with Right Now unless you Think about it?

Talks with 'Sailor' Bob Adamson

Books Published By ZEN Publications

Advaita, the Buddha and the Unbroken Whole
Zen Publications, Mumbai, 2000

It So Happened That...: The Unique Teaching of Ramesh Balsekar
Zen Publications, Mumbai, 2000

Sin and Guilt: Monstrosity of Mind
Zen Publications, Mumbai, 2000

Meaningful Trivialities from the Source
Zen Publications, Mumbai, 2000

The Infamous Ego
Zen Publications, Mumbai, 1999

Who Cares?!
Zen Publications, Mumbai, 1999

The Essence of the Bhagavad Gita
Zen Publications, Mumbai, 1999

Your Head in the Tiger's Mouth
Zen Publications, Mumbai, 1997
Advaita Press, Redondo Beach, California, 1998

Consciousness Writes
Zen Publications, Mumbai, 1996

The Bhagavad Gita—A Selection
Zen Publications, Mumbai, 1995

Ripples
Zen Publications, Mumbai, 1994

Consciousness Speaks
Advaita Press, Redondo Beach, California, 1992
Zen Publications, Mumbai, 1996

What's wrong with Right Now
unless you Think about it?

Talks with 'Sailor' Bob Adamson

Edited by Gilbert Schultz

ZEN
PUBLICATIONS

Published by
ZEN PUBLICATIONS
24/D1, Sagar Soceity,
S.V.P. Nagar, MHADA, 4 Bungalows,
Andheri (W), Mumbai 400 053. INDIA.
TeleFax.: 91 022 634 1615
eMail: zenlinks@vsnl.com
www. zenpublications.com

Printed by

ANITA PRINTERS

Credits:
Front & Back Cover Original Design: Gilbert Schultz
Photographs, Transcription & Editing: Gilbert Schultz
Layout & Design: Red Sky Designs, Bombay

ISBN: 81-88071-11-0

Preface

In 1995 I was given a book called 'I am That'—transcriptions of meetings with Sri Nisargadatta Maharaj. I was drawn to read it almost every day for four years. Maharaj's words were penetrating and revealed a profound understanding. I recognized an echo of 'knowing' in the wisdom which presented itself over and over in the answers from Maharaj. It was clear to me that he had found or had been given a key to understanding. This was my longing—'to understand.' The search for a living teacher took me to India. There I attended Ramesh Balsekar's daily meetings. These meetings confirmed that what I was seeking was much closer than I thought. These one to one conversations produced a dramatic shift in my consciousness which lasted for weeks. I would say that the simple fact of it was that the 'thinking mind' had been exposed. I have a deep respect for his teaching. It was in the home of Ramesh Balsekar that I made a new and lasting friendship with a fellow Australian, Chris Dale, who told me about 'Sailor' Bob Adamson, an Australian who had been with Nisargadatta in the 70's. After returning to Australia, Chris sent me a tape of one of Bob's meetings.

The content of this tape touched me with its clarity and directness—despite the murky quality of the audio copy.

I scribbled down notes from the meeting, seemingly for my own purposes. A complete transcript of the meeting eventuated and the book you hold in your hands is an extended version of that jotting of notes.

In his clear and direct way Bob showed me that the

answer is not in the mind.

When the self investigation truly begins, we recognize the significance of these new ways of looking at ourselves. The teaching transforms or dissolves erroneous ideas and concepts and the mind is freed from the burden of heavy thoughts. In this teaching, nothing is required from us, just an openness to 'see' for ourselves.

We are this 'knowing presence' and as the focus shifts away from the habitual identification with the mind and body, there is a revealing of the clarity that has always been here. The habitual story of 'me' is an obstacle to the realization of our true nature. When this 'me' is seen to be just a 'bunch of ideas'—it loses its hold.

This teaching heralds a transformation of mind.

The elimination of all that is false is just in the 'seeing' of the false as being false—then 'the true' is clearly present.

The concepts expressed in this book point towards understanding, not 'my' understanding or 'your' understanding but Understanding which is Truth itself. In this 'teaching' it is seen that the teaching itself is merely the constant pointing to One Reality, One Truth and One Understanding, One Being.

These words: Reality, Truth, Understanding, Being, Presence, Awareness, Consciousness are not separate—in essence it is all One—Non Dual—One without a second. The mind can't grasp or conceptualize it.

This 'teaching' speaks of the unspeakable, it constantly points us towards the recognition of clear presence awareness and it heralds 'the end' of the search.

When the search ends—all that is necessary unfolds naturally and effortlessly.

However, it could also be said that many seekers do not resonate with this open and direct teaching. Some of us are moved by the message and others seemingly not.

Bob's direct way of pointing to this subtle fact of one's own 'conscious being presence' is rarely found in the spiritual search. It could be said that what is 'true' in us resonates with truth when it is heard or read, it 'rings a bell'.

If you are touched by the content of this book, I highly recommend a visit to him. At present, meetings are held three times a week at his home in Melbourne, Australia.

Beyond thought is Awareness of Being.
This, when truly recognized is a revelation.
This is the key to the 'heart of the matter'.
The heart of the recognition is this One—without a second.

I can assure the reader that within the dialogues found in this book, there are revelations that seem extraordinary at first, then they become a certainty.

The concepts help to point it out—then it is seen.

I can't find the words to describe what a remarkable being that Bob is. I can say that I will be forever grateful for his appearance in Life.

Gilbert Schultz
Sydney, Sept 2001

Note of Thanks

I am deeply thankful to Bob and Barbara for welcoming me so warmly into their home on many occasions while working on this book. These times were full of laughter, openness and a relaxed loving atmosphere. The teaching revealed its clarity in this presence.

Special thanks to Joji and Lena for assisting with corrections to the manuscript and to Anne-Marie Clarke, Eckhard Werner, John Smith, Chris Dale and Janette for their continued support and extraordinary friendships.

Gilbert Schultz

Introduction

I AM not speaking to any 'body'.
I AM not speaking to any 'mind'.
I AM speaking to THAT I AM that I AM,
to that PRESENCE AWARENESS,
that expresses through
the mind as the thought I AM
just THIS and NOTHING else.

That is the direct and immediate introduction to the natural state, the actuality 'That Thou Art', expressed through 'Sailor' Bob Adamson to seekers who have found their way to him over the past 24 years.

Bob's search ended one day in 1976 when he was in the presence of Sri Nisargadatta Maharaj, a much revered *Jnani* who functioned always from the 'natural state'.

Nisargadatta told Bob that the greatest help that can be given to anyone is to take them beyond the need for further help.

Bob says: '… this Nisargadatta did by pointing to the reality, the actuality, THAT I AM. Now, I abide as THAT'. So, as the opportunity arises, Bob passes on this message to those who are attracted by this wisdom.

❧

What you are in essence is 'self shining pure intelligence'. The very idea of shining implies a movement. Movement is energy so I call it 'pure

9

intelligence energy'.

It is shining through your eyes—you cannot say what it is—and you cannot negate it either. It is 'no thing'—it cannot be objectified. It ever expresses as that living vibrant sense of presence, which translates through the mind as the thought 'I am'. The primary thought 'I am' is not the reality. It is the closest the mind or thought can ever get to reality—for reality to the mind is inconceivable—No Thing.

Without the thought 'I am'—Is it stillness? Is it silence? Or is there vibrancy about it?

A livingness, a self-shining-ness.

All these expressions are mental concepts or pointers towards it but the bottom line is that you 'know' that you are. You cannot negate that 'knowing' that you are—it is not a dead, empty, silent stillness. It is not about keeping the mind silent but seeing that what is prior to the mind is the very livingness—it is very subtle.

Then—when you see that that is what you are— then the very subtleness expresses itself. That is the uncaused joy. Nisargadatta puts it beautifully—he puts it in the negative 'There is nothing wrong any more'.

We think that we have to attain something and then stay there.

Realize that you have never left it at any time. It is effortless—you don't have to try or strive or grasp or hold ...You are That.

Contents

'All you need is to be aware of being, not as a verbal statement but as an ever present fact'.

—Shri Nisargadatta Maharaj

1

The Answer is not in the Mind

The following text is transcribed from recorded meetings.

(The following lines are from a text given to be read by those present)

'There will never be any more God than there is now. Never more of good, wholeness, abundance, perfection, infinity than at this present moment. Living in this moment of 'IS-ness' the next moment unfolds as a continuity of Grace'.

Bob: There is never any other 'time' than right now.

Question from visitor: Can time exist?

It is always Presence. When you are thinking about it, it is *presently*.
   Time is a mental concept.

Q: Who wrote this text?

In the context that it was written, it does not matter who wrote it.

Q: How and why did the One become many?

In non-duality, in One without a second, not even the One, just pure presence awareness, how can the experience know itself?
It is complete, it is whole, it is perfect.
To re-experience that—it puts a veil of ignorance over itself as it vibrates into different patterns with experiences and expressions through these different patterns. Then it turns around and comes to know itself again. Returning to its completeness.
The Hindu tradition calls it 'The Dance of Shiva'
The Play of God, *Lila* or the 'Sport of God'.
So, in reality, nothing has ever happened.
Patterns of energy appear—it is still the same Intelligence energy.
Patterns appear just the same as the reflections appear in the mirror.
What has happened to the mirror?

Q: Nothing!.... is there one mind or are there several minds?

There can only be One Mind, if there is any such thing as Mind. Mind is an appearance also! So it can appear as 'many'.

Q: Do I know myself through the mind or is it independent of the mind?

The only instrument we have is the mind. So it has to be understood that you can never grasp it with the mind. Because IT contains the mind.
The mind can never contain IT.

Q: What about the feeling or the thought 'I am'?

That is the primary thought from which all the dualism appears. As soon as there is 'I am' there must be 'you' or the 'other'.
That idea 'I am' is the cause of all our *seeming* problems.
That sense of presence is expressing itself through the mind, but prior to that thought, you know that *you are*—don't you?
You are not thinking 'I am' constantly all the time, are you? You know that you are sitting there, you are aware of being present—continually.

Q: What about when I am in deep sleep? I am not aware.

The mind is in abeyance in deep sleep. But that effortless functioning is still going on. The mind is not there. That functioning is still breathing you.
It is still causing the blood to flow around through the body. The fingernails continue to grow. All these do not stop because the mind is not there.
Consciousness or the mind stirs in that deep sleep and you start to dream before you are awake. In this dream you create a world and you see yourself taking an active part in it. It might be in a town, a city, a room or out in the country. You can dream of all sorts of things. There can be other people there, could be cars, animals or anything and you see yourself taking an

15

active part. Yet that body has not moved from the bed. All of this seeming world has been taking place in that little space between your ears. If you continued to dream every night and the dream continued on from the night before just as in the waking state appears to do, could you tell the difference between the dream state and the waking state?

So is the world anything other than mind?

What substance has the mind? What substance has a thought got?

That 'I am' thought is what you believe yourself to be. Can the mind stand on its own?

If you were not conscious—if that consciousness was not there, could you have a single thought?

Q: I don't know!

Well you just said that even in deep sleep, you were not aware of it. No thoughts. The mind is dependant on consciousness or awareness or whatever you want to call it, that pure intelligence energy. So that must be *primary*, that must be the reality, not the 'I am' thought, not the 'me' as such.

Q: So is consciousness dependant on anything else?

That is also just a movement in Awareness.

All this world appears in that Consciousness.

All this world is the content of Consciousness.

So, it can not be anything other than Consciousness.

There is nothing that you can think of, conceive of, perceive or postulate outside of Consciousness.

Even if you are talking about other universes or other solar systems. The moment you think about or

16

talk about them, you have brought them into Consciousness.

When that 'thinking and talking' consciousness is out of the road, there is that pure intelligence there, it just shines of itself.

Q: So is consciousness a part of the universal?

The whole thing is the universal, if you look at it closely, no parts.

Awareness or the Absolute, Consciousness, Mind are one and the same thing in different aspects.

Like with water—you have water vapor or steam then the liquid state of water and then there is ice. These are three different aspects of the one thing, water.

So, it still never changes from that non-dual One without a second. Grasp that fact and stay with that, it does not matter what appears—it is still only the One.

Then that sense of separation can no longer be there.

Q: How do we account for the population increase then? If All is One and nothing can be taken away or nothing can be added, how do we explain the population increase?

Well, it can vibrate into myriads and myriads of patterns.

Q: So does that imply that something else is losing?

No. What is the something else? It is still that One and the same intelligence energy!

You see, they say that this universe as we know it started off as an atom or a quark or something minute. All this energy started from that. From our point of view, it is still expanding and that original so called beginning is 15 billion years ago.

In a drop of water there are myriad forms of life.

Within that life there is more life on a finer scale.

Going out into space to where the Earth is just a speck, that is another, quite different point of reference. Now, where is it all judged from?

It is still all within that One. To get a true judgment of it, you would have to step outside of it.

That is impossible!

The time scale differences between the life in the drop of water, the life as we experience it and the life out there in deep space is vastly different. The life of a cell could not possibly conceive of our life of a hundred years.

It is all relative to the reference point taken.

Our reference point is always that 'me' or 'I' but added to it are events or experiences of what happened yesterday or last week or last year or when I was born. These are added to that pure 'I' image. It has built this image that I am a good person or a bad person or I have low self esteem or I am angry or fearful.

You see, that very sense of 'I' is separation.

The very sense of that separation is insecurity.

From being the totality, the Unlimited Potential of Being, we have immediately become an isolated, separate human being with all its limitations. We have built this mental cage around ourselves. Now, from that reference point *(which is based on 'yesterday'—the past)*—everything is judged.

You see that whatever has happened to me is judged from that reference point and I might consider it 'good' or 'bad'.

Our criteria, our reference point is never correct, never true.

18

So, in seeing that, in grasping that, where does it leave you?

It can only leave you right here, right now, aware in the actuality of this moment. *This* is the real! *This* is the real! *This* is the real! *This* is the real!

Q: So, we are whole, complete—nothing to need but just a thought away from being insecure and neurotic.

Yes. If there is no thought, what is wrong with right now?—If you're not thinking about it!

If everything is just as it is—unaltered—unmodified—uncorrected—what is it? It is *just as it is!* **Just One As Is!**

Q: It puts your dreams in a different perspective.
They are real!

Yes, they are very real while you're dreaming them but when you wake up in the morning and see them as a dream, what happens?

Q: I guess basically you dismiss it but sometimes I try to get something from them.

Well do you carry them around all day and say 'that was terrible?' Trying to get something from them would be perpetuating the 'me' or the 'self-centre' which thinks it is going to find an answer.

Q: In the dream, it seems so real, it seems that it actually happened.

It seems so very real but when it is seen as a dream,

19

you are no longer bound by it—just the same as when you see the falseness of that self-centre, that it has no reality either, then you are no longer bound by that and that is the freedom. That is freedom from the *seeming* 'bondage of self'.

Q: I am just thinking that my past experiences are useful if the need arises.

Your memory is there to be used, it is useful. But when memory comes up and carries on and carries on, it starts to use you. It will make you fearful, anxious or depressed or whatever, it is using that self image that you have about yourself. If that 'memory' is not good for it, then 'I don't want to be like this' pops up, so you create another image in the future when you are going to escape from all of this.

As we said before—the mind is the only instrument that we have. The mind is not the enemy just because it causes all the problems. If it is understood clearly, then it is there for what it is meant to be there for. It is a wonderfully creative instrument. But when it believes that it is running the show, then the trouble arises.

The mind is so closely aligned with that Pure Intelligence Energy and because it has never been questioned, it has come to believe that it is the Power— 'I am me'—'I am running the show!'

But when you look at it closely and see that all it is, is an 'image', an idea and on its own it cannot do anything—it relies on that Pure Intelligence Energy.

Now, right now you're hearing and seeing.

Does the hearing say 'I hear?' Does the seeing say 'I see?' What says those things?

Q: The mind!

So in saying those things, the mind has given itself the power. Believing that 'I am doing something'.

Let us look further—does the thought 'I see'—does that see?

Does the thought 'I hear'—does that hear?

So that is the proof that it has no power.

But you're still seeing—you're still hearing—so effortlessly the functioning—the happening is going on.

Effortlessly, that Pure Intelligence Energy is bubbling up through this psychosomatic apparatus, this body-mind, this pattern of energy. You see that the activities are happening.

Q: So, I just have to learn to trust in that.

It is not a matter of trust, it is just coming back and seeing that there is no 'me' to trust. You see that the 'me' is only an accumulation of ideas in your mind, an image based on your past and your conditioning. That pure 'I am' thought is one move away from reality—and because that is pretty hard to grasp on its own, it has added all these other images and ideas and words to it. This has created an image, which seems very real and solid because it has been gone over day after day, week after week from the time we were two years old. It has never been questioned—and that is the only problem. Once it is looked at—the false cannot stand up to the investigation.

That 'I'—that 'me'—that thought can't see, it can't be aware.

It can't breathe you. It can't beat your heart.

It relies on 'that pure functioning' for the thinking it self!

Yet it has come to believe that it has the power.

Without 'thought'—do you ever stop 'being'?

Q: Intellectually I understand completely everything you have said. If I said, again language is a barrier—If I said I want to know what I know intellectually as direct experience, what can you do for me?

Right now, your hearing?

Q: Yes

You're seeing?

Q: Yes.

Feeling?

Q: Yes

That is direct experience!

Is thinking happening?

Q: Yes

Do you hear that tram going by?

Q: Yes

You know immediately it is a tram before it comes into your mind. That is pure intelligence registering everything just as it is.

A split second later you say 'that is a tram' or 'someone coughed'—or 'someone moved'. At that point you have stepped off the **'razor's edge'.**

Prior to that—is the pure registering of everything just as it is. The pure intelligence of itself does not change—it does not move.

It is just like the mirror—it reflects everything just as it is. The difference with the analogy of the mirror is that the mirror has to have stuff outside of it.

Like the Sun—that pure intelligence shines of itself.

All this vibration, this movement of energy is registered just as it is.

The mind comes in with discrimination.

It has preference, partiality or comparison.

It is the nature of the mind to divide.

It is the nature of this manifestation to be in the pairs of opposites.

Could there be silence without sound?

Could there be stillness without movement?

What can you compare them to without the opposites?

Looking at it from this perspective, there is no 'big bad ogre' in all these pairs of opposites.

They are understood for what they are.

So your direct experiencing is right here—right now—presently.

It is always direct experiencing—Full stop!
(*Pause*)

The mind is starting to move away from it with 'What if—such and such' isn't it?

Hearing! Seeing! Feeling! Living! Breathing!
Immediate! It is Immediate!

You will notice that that is always first and foremost. It is only the habit of the mind to 'latch on' and seemingly take you away from it.

But when is that happening? Isn't it presently? You can only be thinking presently. If you are thinking about the past, you must be thinking about it presently.

Thinking about the future—you must be thinking about it presently.

You have **never** moved away from it—it is only seemingly so. A little bit of alert awareness—seeing what is happening—then are you going to be 'bound' by it?

No—because you have seen the falseness of it.

It is not going to stop you going into the 'past' of the 'future'—but you understand it, you have *seen through* the illusion.

Q: So how does a Jnani *function?* (Jnani- Sanskrit word for the 'Knower')

The same as anybody else. Functioning happens... but he knows that there is no 'personal doer-ship'— because it is seen clearly that there cannot possibly be a 'person'.

The idea of a 'person' is an erroneous belief in that sense of separation—the 'me'.

When you see that there is no 'me'—you must know for certain also that there is no 'other'.

It is the same that I know that there is no 'centre' here *(indicating himself)* and I know that there is no 'centre' there *(indicating the questioner).*

So then who is superior? Who is inferior?

What is there to be afraid of? Who do I need to hate or resent?

Q: If there is no centre, how can you have consciousness?

Consciousness is all there is.
There is 'no one' to 'have' consciousness.
The Whole thing is Consciousness.

Q: How can you have the thought that 'I am' which is the separation and activity; there can't be any activity unless you have a centre.

So what about Jesus and Sai Baba, who professed to know 'who' they were and still they acted on this level of consciousness. 'I did this' and 'I did that' but they seemed to know, at least on an intellectual level, they knew who they were. Jesus said that 'My father and I are one' so he knew who he was. If the One is going to express itself and I am a part of the expression and there can't be an expression without thought—which is an illusion of separation. But in my conscious mind I'll have the intellectual awareness that there is no separation and I will experience the experience with this awareness. Is that the best that the mind can do?

You are breathing now—you're seeing—hearing—it is all happening. Now is there any need for a 'me' to allow that to happen?

Q: No

But it is *seemingly so*—isn't it?

Q: As soon as you come into thought it appears to be so.

Yes but when you understand that it is only appearance, is it going to change?

Q: No, I wouldn't think so.

25

You see—you understand that the sky is not blue.

Sky is only space and when you get up in a plane at thirty thousand feet with space all around you, it is still clear and empty, the blue is always further out.

We have believed it to be blue but when you understand that it is not blue you will still see it as the same. But you know full well the truth about it. That is another thing that Christ said: 'Know the truth and the truth will set you free'—that you are not that separate entity!

Now, it experiences and expresses itself through all this diversity.

A dog has the characteristics of a dog. A cat has the characteristics of a cat.

So called human beings have characteristics with the functioning of a human being with their mind and body etc. But knowing full well that you are not that, it is not going to make any difference to the functioning. It is still going to happen. As the Zen text says—'before enlightenment—Chop wood, carry water—After enlightenment Chop wood, carry water'. Before—it is a chore that is happening for 'me' that might like it or might not. Afterwards, it is just part of the functioning, part of the happening.

Q: *But the nature of the thought affects the activity of the world.*

Exactly.

Q: *So this means that your life and what happens depends on your awareness.*

Yes, in other words—you're being lived.

26

Q: So, theoretically, I could walk across Port Phillip Bay and even calm a storm.

Yes, exactly!—That same energy that is contained in that atom which this universe as we know it came from—how many atoms are in that body? Look at the potential energy that is there. Now what stops that?

   'I am a separate human being'. We put the block on it, the block is 'the word'.

Q: So it is not a matter of bringing truth or the One to this level of consciousness? To say that this level of consciousness can't live as One because it is contained in the One. It is the illusion of separation.

Yes, but you are particularizing the consciousness. It is One Universal Consciousness. That is a trap also. You are being lived, so what would you do? Get as much of the blockage and the idea of separation out of the road and let the livingness happen. That is taking the brakes off.

Q: How do you get out of the road? That is like the person trying to do that, isn't it?

Yes, that is right, that is badly put, to say to get yourself out of the road. You just see the falseness and continue to see it.

   Look, investigate and you see the falseness of the so called 'person'.

Q: Yes, I feel like it's the 'person' looking—the person trying to see that there is no 'person'.

You see, what happens is—first off, all there is the 'seeing'. Take that chair over there as an example.

The thought comes up 'I see the chair'. There may be some association with the chair which I don't like, the colour is wrong or whatever. So, the psychological response to the seeing is 'I like it' or 'I don't like it' or whatever. That response is the 'me' or the self centre. So the 'seeing' has then been split into the 'seer'—this image that I have that doesn't like the chair, which is named from memory, it becomes the 'seen' or the 'object'.

Prior to that in the immediacy is just a registration in which there is this 'seeing' which contains the chair and it contains the response also. But the psychological response is the 'me' with all its likes and dislikes—its prejudice and partiality is all that the person is.

If I am aware of that just the same as I am aware of the chair, then what has happened?

In that awareness, is just the 'seeing' because it is seeing not only the 'pseudo object' but the 'pseudo subject' also.

If it is taken on board as 'I am seeing it'—then the 'pseudo subject', believing that it has the power or the reality, is seeing an object.

That is all that ever happens—'objectivity'.

The first object you see is the front of this body.

But we don't take that to be an object—we take that to be the subject.

Q: *What is it that stops an instant transformation when I hear this? How can I hear about this and it doesn't impact? Is it because I am hearing through the mind that filters it or is it just not time?*

None of it 'rang a bell'—as we say?

Q: Oh yeah,

When it is recognized and is not just taken on an intellectual basis, it is recognized to be true—then that is yours from then on. It may not come up for a day or a week but at some particular time it will come up in your livingness and you'll say 'Ah! That's what that is' and you will know it in your own understanding and it may be the same words or different words altogether. With the 'knowing' of it, the recognition of it and the understanding of it—then it is grasped. This will continually go on. If you can do the same with what I have been saying about the self centre—seeing the falseness of it—that it is only an image—that it has no substance—then that strips it right away.

Even though the mind will continue to think the way that it always has. As long as you are embodied, you're going to have that mind.

It is still going to think in the same way. It can't think in any other way than in the pairs of opposites.

In understanding it—you are no longer bound by it. The old habit patterns will come and catch you for awhile but they have lost their intensity and the further you go along, the less they bother you.

Q: Is it correct to say the following? For the appearance of movement—the physical movement of the energy that we observe—for that movement to appear, there must be something that is rock hard solid for it to appear on?

It is not rock hard solid, it is just like the reflecting surface of the mirror. Like the Sun shining in the sky— now can the Sun know darkness? No—if it can't know darkness—can it know light?

No!—Yet it shines of itself. Its nature is to shine. Now the nature that is emanating from that body-mind organism—it is shining through your eyes, it is hearing through your ears—it is that same intelligence energy—its nature is to shine. We put the clouded mind upon it and become poor depressed, anxious souls.

So allow that essence within you to shine.

Let it shine through your eyes and light your eyes up—let it permeate your whole physical being with its healing essences.

It was there before the brain was even formed. It is vibrating and pulsating through you now. It is one and the same energy. It is that All Presence.

Q: How do I get to it? I know I am already it, how do I perceive it through the mind?

Just see the falseness of the 'I', then you are left with it.

Q: I can understand that but it is not happening. Can you make it happen right now?

It is happening right now!

Your hearing, you're seeing the functioning is going on as pure experience right now.

The trouble arises because you are looking for something to grasp it with the mind and say 'this is it'.

You see, you are looking for an experience in the mind to say 'ah! That's it' and then all you do is tuck that away in your memory and you go along on your merry way looking for something else.

When they say in the Gita—'The fire can't burn it—the water can't drown it—the wind can't dry it and the sword can't cut it'. What does that mean? Why can't the sword cut it? Because IT contains all of those things.

Now you will **never** find the answer in the mind.

IT contains the mind.

The mind can never contain IT.

As we pointed out earlier—before that thought 'I am' comes on to you—are you aware?

Q: Yes.

Right! **That's it!** But you can't say anything about it. That doesn't *sound right* to the mind because the mind is looking for some experience. It is very subtle.

Q: Why can't I 'stay' with that?

When do you move away from it?

Q: When the mind comes in.

When is that happening?

Q: What do you mean?

When the mind comes in—isn't it *presently*?

Q: Yes.

Well, you are still with it. You are only seemingly moving away from it.

What 'past' is there unless you think about it?

Q: Yes—there is none.

31

There is just now! So you see that past is an 'idea' or an 'image' in your mind of a moment ago or last week or yesterday but it is happening presently. You only imagine that you have moved away from now.

The same with your anticipating and imagining tomorrow or a moment away.

Q: So how do I stop this imagining?

It is not necessary to stop it if you understand what is happening—if you understand that it is still presence.

When is it happening? Just ask yourself that question. When is all this happening? The obvious answer is that it can only be happening presently. So is it anything other than presence?

The 'happening' itself is movements of energy. Thoughts are subtle sound. Sound is energy and energy is just vibration.

So it is that Omnipotence, that All Power. It is Omnipresence, it is All Presence. And the 'knowing' of that, the awareness of it, knowing that I am, the pure 'knowing' is the All Knowing, the Omni-Science.

It does not mean to know this or know that—it is just Pure Knowing.

Pure knowing is the Totality of knowing.

Are you not that right now? Aware of being present.

In the Hindu terminology it is *Sat-Chit-Ananda*.

Awareness-Being-Loving.

You are aware of being present.

And you 'love to be'. Full stop.

You are aware of being present.

Anything else is still happening presently.

Just the focus needs to move back a little bit and see.

Instead of focusing on what we have been used to

focusing on 'in the head'—just pause for a minute and see the difference between that pure intelligence, the registering of everything and the thinking about it.

Realize that you're hearing those cars go by while you're listening to me *(you're hearing sounds as you read)* probably with your full attention, you are still hearing and seeing other things and it is still being registered.

Try listening in here—in here.

The first seeing is formless. In that formlessness there are still forms appearing out there.

The first hearing is silence. But there is still hearing out there.

You are that formless silent pure being.

Very subtle. Stay with it!

To the mind this is very boring. 'Oh gee! I can't live in silence and stillness!'

Q: It is almost too simple for my mind to grasp.

Exactly! Well let the mind go. It is that simple, so simple that we miss it. Pure simplicity itself.

Stay with that subtleness, that silence and stillness and you will see things and understand the ancients when they say 'the peace that passes all understanding'.

Because it could not be understood by the mind.

There is no 'peace of mind'. It is the nature of the mind to chatter. You are not that chatter. The mind oscillates between the pairs of opposites.

Peace is where the mind is not.

Q: Is there any way to stop this chatter?

No. Do you chatter? Understand and watch it.

If you haven't got a vested interest in it, what is

going to happen? It is going to die down.

You see, when the chatter starts and I attribute it to 'me' and 'I want this' or 'I don't like that' or 'he said so and so' and 'blah, blah, blah, blah'—I have a vested interest in it. Now in that vested interest what is happening? The energy of 'I' and 'this'—the 'I' is a thought and the 'this' is a thought but that energy is opposed to itself. It is a dissipating energy—it is in conflict with itself. But if I understand that there is no centre here and that it is just chatter and I am aware of it then there is no 'me' that wants anything out of it.

There is nothing resisting it. It is just what is.

Then there is no energy going into it.

Now can a thing live without energy? No!

So in the watching of it—in the awareness of it—without bothering about it—in seeing it for what it is—it is false—it is going to die down of its own accord.

So there is no need to try and stop it. In trying to stop it the mind will be in conflict with the mind. That will get you into all sorts of trouble which it has done until now.

Q: *So, how do we stop? I see that chatter but I am still giving it value.*

Well keep watching it and ask yourself who is this 'me' that is giving it value? Until it comes up that you see—that this 'me' is only an idea.

Where is this centre? Where does this so called me start?

Look and try and find a centre or a spot in your body which you believe is 'me'. Or in your mind—which you believe is 'me'. Look as hard as you like—if you can find it—you come and tell me!

I know for certain that there is no particular place in this body or this mind that I can say that this is where I begin; this is where it all starts.

So in your own looking you will find that the false cannot stand up to investigation. You are not the hand—you are not your ear—you are not your nose. There is no particular spot where you can say this is where I began. Have a look at the body—it started off as a single sperm and a single ovum, which were the essences of the food that your mother and father ate. Where is that cell? That would be the centre that would be the start of it all but that cell has doubled and redoubled and it is long gone.

From another angle—am I this mind? The mind is just composed of thought. Which particular thought am I? Am I this 'I' thought but where is that 'I' thought if I am deeply asleep or unconscious? It is not there! That would be the finish of me if I was that 'I' thought. But the breathing is still happening—the functioning is still happening—there is no centre there.

So when the chatter goes on and you see that there is no centre to attribute it to—then it must lose its hold.

It becomes laughable.

Q: *So, even if there is no chatter, in this consciousness, one is living and being, one consciously knows that one is an expression of the One and it is an illusion of duality that is creating an experience for the One to know itself...*

No, if you say it's a delusion you're putting the separation on it. If it is just What Is—you can't say anything about it at all.

35

Q: *What my consciousness says is that I don't experience it on levels that I know other people do experience it. I heard a well known Swami talk a number of years ago and he said that with yoga practices, with meditation practices, one gets to know the mind. To use the mind to go beyond the mind. It seems to me that Consciousness cannot know anything outside of Consciousness.*

That seems to be the dilemma. Our interaction here is on the level of consciousness—so wouldn't it be the technique to learn how to be still and know that I am God? Wouldn't meditation practices be the best you could do to get there, if there is somewhere to get?

Whatever this Swami or anybody experienced, it is still not it.

The so called transcendental states are still not it.

See it does not matter whether there is silence here or chatter because both to me are still experiences.

But that 'pure knowing', which they both appear on, that pure registration of everything—that is beyond experience. That is Pure Experiencing.

If it is understood with the mind that no matter what experience appears—can never be it.

The answer is not in the mind.

So then you are not concerned with wanting to experience some so called ultimate state or non-state.

You just stay with the subtleness of 'being now' and see what is in that and see what appears from that—the uncaused joy—the uncaused happiness and the pure compassion that comes up.

As soon as they are expressed through the mind, that is the 'name' that you give them but you cannot say I am experiencing this.

Q: No—the Swami said that it was necessary not to be a prisoner of the mind. But he talked about techniques then— to become more aware of the mind—to start to know the nature of mind.

Yes, well there are all sorts of techniques; I can give you some techniques if you want them.

If you can grasp what has been said here and take it away with you—it is going to hatch—it is going to bear fruit.

Q: Yes, well that is what I experience, to know something on an intellectual level is one thing and I relate to what you said about starting to own something and then it starts to become your truth and then you change. That is a process I am familiar with.

Well then you know because it has already happened to you. That is why you are familiar with it, so it will happen again. It has brought you from other places to here. Despite ourselves, it takes you where you have got to go. Not that you have ever been anywhere.

How is it all sitting with you? *(to a regular visitor)*

Q: These two are saying exactly the opposite, they say that intellectually that they know but they don't experience it.

I would rather say that you are experiencing it right now…— but intellectually you don't know. Does that make sense?

Yes, that is well put—**intellectually you don't recognize that you are the experiencing itself.**

Q: Yes and that's it, there is nothing to know. The mind keeps on wanting to know, wanting to know. It is causing a problem by wanting to know.

Exactly! And when you understand that no matter how far you go, the answer is not in the mind, what would you do? Full stop. I am not going to bother looking there anymore.

Q: But I do keep looking there.

Yes, because that is habit. It is understandable because we have been conditioned from an early age—day in, day out, just like the smoker reaches for a cigarette, whether he is thinking about it or not.

The habit is there. But in seeing it for what it is, the habit is starting to be broken.

Q: So, if a new born is in the company of say someone like you, would it also continue on like us or would it know instantly?

Well, it soon takes on the conditioning of the world. The young child is often laughing and doing things spontaneously and quite naturally. But after awhile at about the age of two, they learn to scowl, to stamp a foot and you see the conditioning starting to form. Then they go off to school where they learn different 'looks', putting on little tantrums and so it goes on.

Q: That can't be stopped?

No.

Q: You can really only know the world through the mind,

through the word?

Yes, but know it for what it is and there is no problem.

Q: But you have to experience it to know it don't you?

Yes, you're continually experiencing it—but just know it for what it is—you find that things just happen. You just sail through it. You see so many people on the tram or bus or train, locked in their heads, their eyes down, they are not looking around at the trees or traffic or the others on the tram. It becomes almost palpable.

Q: It is like your own little private prison.

Exactly! The bondage of self. The cage we have built around ourselves—made by words.

Q: We are very fortunate to come across this other view.

Well, if it happens that way for this so called particular human being. What brought you here?

Q: What do you think it is that brings us Bob?

Well it is that same consciousness, that same essence that so called particular entity returning back to its own completeness. It has experienced itself and expressed itself in its ignorance, now it has got the joy of coming home.

Q: What I understood about twelve months ago, with prayer and meditation, where you allow the light to come in. You break away from that self enough to allow something to come in—to stop depending on it—to break that sense of bondage. I know with my experience, I got to the point where I was not going to live any more. Something had to give. We are talking about the bondage of self, I know that the bondage of self kills. I have lived the life of addiction so I know that. So what is it? I know what it is for me, but what is it that draws people? I always believed that it was because someone prayed for me. But I don't know what I believe now.

Love is another term for light. Christ says 'I am the light of the world'. That is that 'I am'—that sense of presence. By what light do you see the world?

Q: Through the energy I guess.

Exactly, so light or love is that energy expressing through that body-mind organism as that light.

That light has sort of pierced the cloud. From that so called point of view of that body-mind entity that is so clouded over it could not grasp it within its own orbit. So it manufactures something else, like the fellowship for instance, then it will bring you to someone 'who knows'.

The whole essence is functioning and it puts in your way what is necessary to bring you in a full circle. It might be a person, a book and 'Bang'! It starts you on your way home.

Q: I was in the Fellowship for 12 years and I had no concept of a higher power. I was—the ego and it 'Run a-mock' and then suddenly I had a spiritual experience just 'come upon me'.

It took that time. At that particular time there was the

openness or a letting go was there or the self was out of the way and the fruit had ripened at that particular point.

Not all fruit ripen at the same time, some may never ripen.

Q: Could you quicken the process?

We told you before—**that you are already there!**

Q: I am going around in circles.

Well. Full Stop—did you stop? Stop thinking?

Hear the bird singing? Are you thinking about that? It is happening! It just is!

The conditioning as we have just said is that the mind wants to know. The mind in wanting to know will perpetuate itself. It will go down every direction it can find. So whichever direction you go in—you're still in the mind! There is only one way to get out of that is—Full Stop.

In that instant of stopping, there is clarity, there is just what is. Just a second later it starts up again—but if you see it in that instant—the instance will widen.

In the registration of what is, just as it is, right here—right now. Without any modification, alteration or correction—that is what is.

What could modify it—alter it—or correct it?

Only the mind. Only a thought or feeling.

If I ask you what is wrong with right now, without thinking about it, what would you say?

You have to pause for a moment—and realize that if there is no thought there—there is nothing wrong.

In that instance you have also stopped it.

That is it. That is where it is. That may seemingly be only instantaneous at the moment.

But if that sinks in often enough—that there is nothing wrong unless I am thinking about it.

Then even if the thinking is going on, you know that you don't have to take any delivery of the thinking.

That is the cause of all my problems.

In that split second—without that thinking—I still existed, I still was!

Focus more with that. The mind is not the 'Be-all and End-all' that we have believed it to be.

That we can't live without it or can't exist without it. We have placed so much importance in it.

See that it is not so important, though it is a wonderful creative instrument, it is not so important.

The livingness is going on effortlessly—right now.

Go along those lines—investigate yourself and see.

It will hit you 'that's right! It is not so important.

Then it starts to lose its hold—you will never be the same again.

When ever you get the chance throughout the day— question—stop and see. **What is wrong with right now if I don't think about it.**

Is the 'I' seeing? Is the 'I' aware? Or is the 'me' seeing or is the 'me' aware?

Or does the eye say 'I see' and does the ear say 'I hear'.

Realize that the functioning is happening effortlessly without any 'me' involved.

It is only the thought 'I' that comes up and says 'I see' but the thought cannot see.

So you see what an error the mind is telling you.

In seeing that, you can never believe it again.

If it tells you erroneous things in that respect, then

it must have told you a lot of other erroneous things. It told me that I needed to drink at one stage—it had me believing it so much that I became obsessed with it and I didn't think I could live without it. For many years it had me believing that I needed to smoke. When it was really questioned and looked into—I need neither of those.

The mind can tell you erroneous things because the reference point is a dead reference point.

It is based on 'Yesterday'. Question it continually and see whether it is telling you correctly or whether it is based on some past dead image.

Do that for a little while and you will see. Those beliefs won't be given any credence any more. Yet when the mind is utilized—it is a wonderfully creative instrument.

"The only instrument that that Pure Intelligence has got is this thinking mind. Intelligence functioning through the mind is nothing but the Pure Intelligence vibrating into a pattern, which we call thought."

෪

2

Are you the mind?

As you all know, we talk about Non Duality here.

The only reality you are absolutely certain of—is the fact of your own Being.

First off—we would suggest that you just relax.

Don't try and grasp what is being said necessarily with the mind. Because, as you see—or as you will see—the mind is the problem.

Just relax and be receptive, because the words that are coming out here presently are coming from that intelligence energy.

If the mind is not acting as the cloud (*as an obstruction*)—what will be receiving those words is that same intelligence energy. Then what is apperceived or grasped or understood—will come up through the mind at the appropriate time, which will be presently, at the appropriate place which will be here and now.

Then the appropriate activity will take place from that.

So, that is what we suggest happens here.

No one—right here, right now, can negate their own beingness. Each one of us knows that 'I am'.

That 'I am' is not much to grasp on to—if it is just purely and simply 'I am'.

So it adds to itself all the events, experiences and conditioning and forms an image and an idea and this idea or image is believed to be what I really am—and all our problems arise from that.

That is so because the very idea of 'me'—separates 'me' from 'other than me' or 'non-me'.

Separation is isolation, it is loneliness, it is fear, it is insecurity—it is vulnerable.

This is what we continually do, we separate and we continually search for wholeness or security or happiness.

It is not our fault, it is not our parents fault.

It is the way we have been conditioned.

The way they were conditioned.

You see, if I believe that I am separate, an individual, a separate entity and person, then I am insecure.

So at the first level, the family level, I try and have a warm and loving family around me to make me feel secure.

Then there is the tribal level and if I can be 'in with the tribe'—then I will be more secure. Then, there is the nation—and nations go to war with nations over that same self centered-ness or insecurity—divisions and separations.

And yet all the great scriptures, all the great religions, all the great traditions will tell you that God, if you like to use that term, is One without a second, it is non-dual, it is—**just this present awareness.**

Just this—and nothing else.

Some of the Christian scriptures will tell you 'I am the Lord thy God, there is none other'. Another term they use is that God is Omnipresence, Omniscience and Omnipotence. It is All Power, All Presence and All Knowing. And they mean *exactly that*. Non Dual—One without a second—Presence awareness.

Now where does that leave room for a 'you' or a 'me' or anything else?

If there is a 'you' and a 'me' in this all power and all presence and all knowing—that means that it is not 'all knowing', it is not all presence and it is not all power. So, from that point of view, all of this manifestation can be nothing other than That.

And that is one of the great sayings from the Hindu tradition—**'Thou Art That'**.

Because there is nothing other than **That**.

'I Am That' is another great saying.

Is there anyone here right now that is not that presence?

You are present—right here and right now.

Is it your presence? Is it my presence? Is it each one of us as individual presence?

Or is it All Presence?

Is there anyone here that is not 'knowing' that—right now? Is it your knowing? Is it my knowing?—Or is it somebody else's knowing?

Or is it Omniscience—All Knowing.

Knowing implies an activity and all activity is energy. You hear the cars going by, you hear the other sounds in the room. You see the movements in the room.

All sound—all movement, is it yours?—Is it mine? Or is it somebody else's? Activity or energy is power.

Is it Omnipotence—All Power?

47

Just have a look at this and see it clearly. Then ask yourself 'who am I?' What is this 'I' or 'me' that thinks itself to be separate?

Where does it start? Where does it finish? What is it?

You see the search as I said previously is always going on 'out there'

'Out there' is where we have been conditioned to look.

Gathering something that will make me secure—that will make me whole—it will make me happy. So if it is not in the family, the tribe or the nation, then it is in a better job—more money—better relationship—a good house—all sorts of things out there—the more I accumulate, the more secure I will be.

Or—if I go on some spiritual search, I will become 'realized' or 'enlightened' or 'whole' and complete. All anticipated to happen in some future time.

I can go on all through my life doing that. If it doesn't look like it is happening in this life, then what do I do?

If I am a Christian, I conceptualize a God somewhere who has a Heaven somewhere in the future. If I am not doing too well 'here' and I say my prayers and do a few good deeds, I will finish up 'there' at some future time. All that is, is conceptualization! An idea of some future time, of some future place and some future Deity or Being that will make it right for me.

Or if I belong to an Eastern religion—I will reincarnate—at some future time!

I will have another life! Never realizing that there is only Now! (*Omnipresence*).

Never looking to see what it is that is going to have this other life—to see what it is that has got 'this life' or seemingly thinks it has got this life.

It is quite simple—if you look—you will see it quite clearly and easily.

What does this body consist of? The essence of the food. Where does the food come from?

It comes from the Earth—the Earth from the Fire.

Fire, Water, Air and Space. It is nothing but the Elements.

Where do the Elements come from?

Well, in that vibration, that movement, these things appear.

And so they are nothing other than energy.

That one energy—omnipotence.

The mind is the same thing.

What is the mind? The mind is nothing but thought!

Thought is subtle sound. Word is sound.

What is sound? Vibration.

What is vibration? Energy!

Omnipotence again—appearing as different.

So, I have never ever moved away from it. I have never ever separated.

So it is foolish for me to try and seek wholeness, completeness or whatever at some future time.

If I look at the mind again and ask myself 'What past is there?' Unless I think about it!

What future is there? Unless I think about it!

In looking at that, I can see clearly that there is no past and—there is no future unless it is thought.

I can bring yesterday's events—from my memory—into my mind right now—but they are not the actual.

For instance, I met so and so yesterday, spoke to him and shook his hand etc...

Well is it the same today? I may have forgotten some

small details and added some that weren't there.

So I have made up this present concept or idea of what went on.

Or, I anticipate or imagine the future—I imagine something in the future—which I can get fearful about or ecstatic about.

But look closely—when is all this taking place?

Isn't it taking place presently?

Can there be any other time that it takes place in?

You can say, 'Oh yes! It took place yesterday'.

But when are you saying that?

Isn't it presently?

Or you can say tomorrow is going to be a different day.

When are you saying and thinking that?

Isn't it presently?

Now it is all happening in that presence.

Is it any different from that presence?

That Omni-Presence, All Presence.

You can say All is God—wrong!

God is All! All is only an illusion. All is not.

All is only a word.

A word is not the real. It has never been real.

Water—water—water—you can't drink the word—water.

These words—these words! Are nothing! In the same way. But isn't there Omnipotence, that vibration, that movement of energy?

Is it going on here? There? Or anywhere in particular? You can feel it. The hearing of the word right now—is a vibration. That which is hearing it is vibrating and pulsating. The heart is beating, the lungs are expanding and contracting. Feel the energy moving around in that body.

Is anyone not knowing that they are? The omnipotence is functioning.

When is it all happening?

Presently—and omnipresence is functioning.

Seeing this, understanding this, I can see how I have been caught.

I can see how I have put a seeming limitation upon myself. I put a cage—that does not exist—around myself.

You have seen the bird in a cage that has been there for many, many years?

You can open the door of that cage and the bird is not going to fly out straight away.

You can leave the door open for days but the bird will not take that step to fly out of it.

We point out here and continually point out the cage. But we say that even the cage is a phantom, it is a false idea. It does not exist.

How many of us step into our freedom by hearing that?

It can be done, right here, right now.

The understanding that you have never been bound—though it may seem that you have been.

What is the limitation that I place upon myself?

First and foremost—it is this idea of being a separate entity, a 'me'.

How does that come about? Purely and simply, if I look at the mind and see how it functions.

Being a movement of an energy, it is a vibration.

Being a vibration, it can only function in the opposites.

Which is the past—memory—or the future—anticipation and imagination.

And in that range it can still only function in the

pairs of opposites. If it is not happy, it is sad. Pleasant—painful, loving—hating, good—bad, positive—negative—whatever. It is still functioning in the pairs of opposites.

And what is it using? Word! Purely and simply word. Often times when things happen, we say 'it doesn't matter'. And when you mean it and it doesn't matter, nothing comes of it.

But if you take some thought or idea aboard and it does matter, that is exactly what it does, it matters and becomes concrete. We beat ourselves over the head with a word. Punish ourselves for the word.

Call something anxiety—show me some anxiety! Show me some fear. That word becomes very real when it is allowed to dance around and vibrate in the mind. What is it referred to? It is referred to a reference point, the 'me' which has felt this feeling before—and it has named it 'fear'—and so as soon as that thought or whatever it is, is seen, immediately comes up the old response from the past which it is referred to, the reference point or the centre.

The centre does not like it, it doesn't want to be here, it wants to escape.

So it immediately resists it, gets in conflict by trying to force it out, change it or do something with it.

So this word that has no power of its own, it has got no substance, it can't stand by itself—it has caused the blood pressure to rise, the goose pimples to rise on the skin, hair stand on end or whatever.

See what 'fear' can do, or any other word.

But if I am not taking that word on board—seeing it for what it is—have understood—that the word can never be the real. It is just let go of!

It appears presently. It is witnessed presently. The

response is witnessed. Nothing further—full stop!

Nothing further happens with it.

The response is not entered into—not trying to change it—not resisting it.

Just seeing it for what it is. It is a word. So what happens?

You see, that energy hasn't taken off—it hasn't started.

Once the energy has started and builds up—then what is it going to do?

The action must follow.

Ever wondered how a cyclone started? It is only energy blowing the air around. It builds up and builds up and look at the damage it can do.

You have seen the storm clouds in the sky with the lightening and thunder, it builds up and builds up and bang! Down comes the rain. It is all released.

Nature does not carry it around like we do.

We get a thought or an idea and the continuity of thought becomes feeling and emotion, it is gone over and over and built on and built on continually.

Look at the damage it does to the physical body.

Look how seemingly real that cage becomes. 'Poor me, I have got no self esteem' or 'I have low self esteem' and it begins to show in the physical form. I walk around with my head down and my shoulders hunched. Look at somebody and wonder—'what they are thinking of me'—or what they are going to do or not do... 'this is going to happen'—'how am I going to survive in the world?'

What has done all this?

Purely and simply, all it is is a word.

A simple vibration...—a vibration that has become a Cyclone, a Tornado within us. It rips us apart—but when has it all happened?

Has there ever been any other time or any other place than right here—right now—presently?

Has it ever moved away from that All Presence— that omnipresence?

So, the word—as I said before—or the body—or the mind—or any of this matter—is nothing.

But presence is that which appears as matter.

I can't move away from that presence. There is nobody to move away.

Any movement, any vibration, anything that is happening, it is that Omnipotence appearing as something other—appearing as the matter—the shape—the form or—as the name we put on it.

'Knowing' that—is the Omniscience—there is only this Omniscience.

What it appears as is nothing other than that appearing as different.

Right here, right now, nobody yet, has negated their beingness or that sense of presence.

Is there anything wrong with that? Unless you think about it.

When I do think something about it—what is thinking?

Can the thought think itself?

Or does thinking appear on that presence—on that awareness?

Is it anything other than presence? Seemingly appearing as different.

Is there any need for any conflict?

Is there any need for any dissipation of energy?

When you look at the mind and see—that the reference point doesn't like this—or wants more of this or whatever—the 'this I don't like' is just an idea or a bunch of words I have—and what it likes or doesn't like is another word—it has a name for it. If it doesn't like it—it is trying to escape from it. If it does like it—then it wants more of it—so there again—there is a struggle—to acquire more.

That energy is seemingly fighting with itself—just through wrong understanding.

All you have to do is look at Nature again—and you will see the opposites in Nature.

They are there. Day-Night, tides coming in, tides going out, seasons coming and going.

You will notice one thing in Nature and that is—that the opposites are not in opposition to each other.

The in coming tide is not fighting with the out going tide.

Winter is not fighting with Summer. Look at your own body—the in coming breath is not struggling with the out going breath.

Your heart is not in conflict within the expansion—it doesn't get half way in expansion and suddenly say 'I am going to contract'.

It is only in the mind that this conflict goes on!

The only reason that it goes on in the mind is the idea of that separate entity, the 'me'.

When that is seen—that there is no separate entity—then who is there to get in conflict with anything?

Things will come—things will go.

That awareness—the alertness—the appropriate activity, takes place spontaneously and intuitively.

It is still going to happen in the pairs of opposites—it might not be good at this moment, it might be bad or something other—if the conflict is not there it will resolve itself quickly and effortlessly.

It may not be the way that 'me' and memory wants

it to be—But I only have to look back over my life and see many things—most of them not the way that this 'me' of memory ever wanted them! Not the way that this 'me' thought they would work out or wanted them to work out.

Most of my life—it has been like that.

Most of the struggle was because this 'me' wanted to change it.

All of the conflict was caused by 'me' and looking back over my life now—I see how that through all the dramas and traumas, I see how beautifully it all fitted in. How it has all fallen into place for this so called entity at this particular spot at this particular time—without that so called 'chatter in the mind' today.

It doesn't mean to say that the chatter doesn't go on—but the chatter has no 'fire' any more.

There may be lots of silence here—and there was a time when I looked for silence and peace—but that was just another experience also—it does not matter.

It is not allowed to 'matter'.

That is so because there is that understanding and knowing that that which all of this has appeared on—that Omniscience that it is—it has never been touched by any of that.

Nothing has ever come near it.

If we must put words to it—it is that still, silent, blissful being-ness—if you like to call it that. Words—which are not the real—but remember what we said at the start.

Never mind the words—just hear and feel the resonance in the word, the vibration, the energy—is it any different from the hearing? Sense and be aware of the vibration where the hearing is taking place.

That 'knowingness'—that awareness of that—still

presently.

Has it ever changed? Are there any questions?

Q: What do you think of meditation in terms of what you said about the chatter in the mind? How do you deal with the chit chat of the mind and the going beyond that chit chat?

If there is awareness, that it is all taking place presently—when are you ever out of meditation?

Q: In the terms of getting to that stage...

When are you saying this?

Q: Well, I am saying.

When are you saying this?

Q: We are talking in the 'now'

Your saying it presently—so where are you going to get to?

You see! You see what you have done? The mind has taken you to some time in the future. This is what we constantly do.

Q: O.K. Yet I still feel that discipline and aspect of working towards something on an everyday basis—because we still need to live lives on a practical everyday basis.

What do you think I do?

Q: So, I am talking about...—how do you actually implement this awareness, in an everyday life in practical terms? And I would say that meditation is a way of connecting and strengthening.

You see, when you say meditation—who is going to connect with it and who is going to implement it in their daily life?

Q: I would say myself.

So, your saying 'me'—so what is this 'me' that is going to do it?
    We pointed out earlier that the 'me' is only an image, an idea.

*Q: I would say that I tend to be dualistic at times.
I recognize that about myself. So...*

Is that you?

Q: The dualistic aspect?

Yes—*(silence)*
    Have a look at the world—the world is dualistic—if it wasn't—in this material manifestation, you would not know that there is a world.
    That is how it appears—but you say that you tend to be dualistic—is that you?

Q: Well, it is kind of my experience in this living process.

Who is the 'me' that is experiencing it? You see what I am trying to get at?
    To bring you back to that original—so that you don't continually jump out into this seeming entity that you

have created.

If you ask yourself this question—who is this happening to?

What would the answer be?

Q: Well it is a projection of myself.

Of 'me', yes, but who is the 'me' that this is happening to?

Where is this 'centre'—where is this reference point, that you are referring all this to?

Q: Well it is a separated me.

Yes—but where is it?

Q: Well, I don't quite understand the question.

Well—where is the centre that you are referring to? The separated 'me'—where is it, what part of it is you? Where is it in your body or your mind—the self centre that you are referring to?

Q: Well, it is in your mind.

Exactly! In your mind—now, are you the mind?

Q: No, but I can't deny the mind does exist in the manifested state.

Yes, but you are not the mind.

Q: I am beyond the mind.

Alright—now you asked the question 'how do you

function in the world?' Now, if you are beyond the mind, you must be aware of what is happening in the mind! See?

Q: *Yes.*

So, what appears in the mind—and what goes on— and the activity that follows on—is that you?

Q: *At times it is unfortunately!* (Laughs)

What I say, is—discard this 'I' that can't say that 'I am beyond the mind'

If you say that you are beyond the mind—that is your actuality—function from that point. The mind is appearing on that—on that pure intelligence that you are.

But—what it is judged from is by the mind itself— an image you have of the past.

Now, being aware of that—are you going to lock into any thing in particular?

If something happens that this reference point 'Jane' doesn't like, you are going to do something about it— your immediately there and you have got to try and change it.

But if that reference point is only mind or word—it is not your reality—what are you going to do about it?

Q: *Leave it alone!*

Exactly! If the energy is not going into a thing, can it live without energy?

No, so it will disappear! Where did it come from in the first place? Where do any thoughts come from?

Q: I would say that that is what meditation really is, it is really working into that very origin of being and learning to work with the mind in terms of it becoming a servant to that higher entity.

But when you meditate, what do you do?

Q: It is still a practice for me, I sit quietly and become aware of a silence and the sounds moving in and out of the silence— and gradually I feel that the energy is lifted and raised in the body until the vibration gets very high.

Yes, but you say 'sit quietly'—now 'who' has got this idea that I am going to sit quietly?
    You get the idea? You say 'I am going to sit quietly and meditate'—so that is the image again—the idea to sit down and we try and still the mind.
    Or we try to watch the thoughts. So that is the 'me' or the reference point.

Q: I would say that it is more or less coming from a reference point in terms of the higher connection.

What is a Higher connection—or what is a Lower connection?

Q: Well, it is where the mind does not come into play and influence. It is beyond the mind.

Did you hear that tram go by just then?

Q: Well, it passed through...

Yes, that was registered on that pure intelligence—just

as it is, right at this moment—just the same as all the other sounds. Your hearing—you're seeing—you're tasting—touching and smelling—these are all registered just as they are!

Now—until I drew your attention to that—the mind did not think a thing about it but it heard it pass through.

So, that pure intelligence is registering everything—just as it is. That is meditation! Meditation is when you are never away from it.

But when you think 'I am going to meditate' or 'I am going to quieten the mind to get a higher connection'—that is where the 'meditators' are using the mind to try and quieten the mind. You can forcibly still it for half an hour and then what goes on—it races away and gets caught in the same rubbish that it was in before!

Q: Do you think so?

I know so! I am talking from experience—but when there is nobody here who is to meditate—what is there to meditate on?

That doesn't leave you a blank—it leaves you **Totally alert in the moment!**
Totally aware!
Where you are not only aware of everything around you, you're aware of what is happening in the mind also—first and foremost.

Are you aware of your thoughts?

Q: Well I am not consciously concentrating on them.

No, but you are aware of thinking?

Q: Yes.

Right—you're aware of those trams going past again?

Q: Yes.

They are objects—you're aware of your thought and your thought is an object also.

So, take it from that view point, that they are both objective—who is the subject?

That which they are all registering on immediately—that pure intelligence.

That—the mind can not grasp—Why? Because—it contains the mind.

So, it is pointless 'trying' to get at it with the mind.

It is just—to see the mind and understand the mind, then you will realize that you are already there.

The registration on that pure intelligence is functioning right now, presently in its fullness, as it has always done. Have you ever moved away from that?

Q: No. I forget about it!

You forget about it! When do you forget about it? Wouldn't it be presently?

Q: Yes.

So what is it? It is still only presence. All the forget-fullness is still only presence, you have never moved away from presence. The mind is not you. You, that Omnipresence is the mind!

Even when you are forgetting about it, it is still there.

Q: *Yes, words.*

That is the bondage, that is what we have trapped ourselves in—and the word is not the real.

Q: *Thank you.*

So, what will you do now?

Q: *Well, I will take my own journey. In terms of us intellectualizing and talking about it and the actual living it and experiencing it—that is where I feel that certain practices are helpful.*

What I was pointing out to you was a direct experience. You see that—and come back to that and you continually see that, that is continually your direct experience.

You are not Jane experiencing this or experiencing that—it is just pure experience—it is happening continually—then the mind interprets this or that experience immediately after the event.

That interpretation is only from the dualistic point of view of the mind—which this manifestation is—but to see that it is pure experience and the functioning is happening, that Jane, as such, has no reality as that seeming person—then the spontaneous functioning happens through that thing which we call Jane—you see that that is what always happens.

Because, if you see that there is no centre now—when did you ever have a centre?

You never did, did you? If there is no centre now then there could never have possibly been one. So, that means that you have never had any personal volition.

The life, the functioning has gone on, even though you thought you were running it, the functioning has happened.

From that point of view, when you understand that— instead of trying to run it and change it or alter it—you go with the flow of it and allow it to happen much freer than what was apparently happening before—with the seeming 'me' putting the 'blockers' and 'stoppers' on.

Q: O.K. How does one perhaps remain true to that aspect when we go about our daily lives—we are using the mind in terms of functioning and then it plays some tricks on us and becomes our master, rather than a servant? In practical terms, how do we work with that aspect of ourselves?

Well, if there is alertness there, if that awareness is acutely alert—then when the tricks start to come up—you see them. You say 'using the mind'—that is what the mind is there for—to be used, it is not the enemy—though it is the cause of all our problems. If it is understood then it is wonderfully creative. All the Art, Architecture, Technology, all the teaching of yoga and whatever you are doing is coming through your mind.

It is only when it is in conflict with the 'me' and the 'other' and seemingly in that separation, that it causes us pain and suffering.

You get trapped in that habit pattern and that is all it is, because over the years you have been conditioned to that way of thinking and believing—it has become habitual.

See the habit of it and you don't fall into the trap of it.

You might get trapped for awhile because that habit pattern is seemingly strong—but if you have seen the falseness of it all—it can never be as intense as it was before—and eventually it won't even bother to come up because the energy won't go into it.

It will be seen—there will be an awareness of it **as soon as it starts.**

'You are prior to the thought. You are not the thought.
Be aware of it. In that registering, in that pure intelligence, it is all being witnessed just as it is'.

ଓଃ

3

Just as it is

The description can never be the described, all we are doing is describing What Is. Right here right now, presently, is what is happening.

Primarily there is that registering of everything.

Just like that mirror on the wall is reflecting everything in front of it, so that essence or intelligence or whatever name you like to call it, is registering everything just as it is. You heard that siren but you didn't have to say it was a siren. You are hearing this voice, seeing the sights in the room, you are feeling your body sitting in the chair. All just as it is—and just as it is—what can you say about it?

You can't say anything at all about it.

From that point of view it either is or is not. The description can never be the described—the What Is.

The thinking is being registered also.

That is discriminated into 'this thought' or 'my thought' or whatever the word might be. Rather—be aware that it all is *just as it is*.

Say you are walking somewhere and you are not naming anything, there is no thinking going on. You are passing houses, trees, picket fences or whatever is in the street. Everything is registering immediately.

You don't have to name each individual thing.

Now, your thoughts might be happening and your mind might be totally involved in those thoughts—yet one piece of concrete paver may be higher than the other but you won't trip over it.

It will be registered immediately and the appropriate steps will be taken over it.

Or if there is a crowd walking in the street, you're not going to bump into everyone. You find yourself avoiding them quite effortlessly without having to think 'I have to dodge around this one'—yet they will be coming from all directions and all places but that intelligence—is registering everything just as it is—and in the moment, the proper activity takes place.

Now the same with thoughts also—as you are going along, your passing this house or the next house and as you are going along, thoughts are happening too.

They are registered just as is. What happens?

The house you have just passed has disappeared from view, or the picket fence you passed is gone— thought is registered just as is also—what has happened to that thought? It is left behind—it also disappears.

One thought might be acted upon, the next may not be.

The only way we can change What is—Is to correct it—modify it—or alter it in some way or form—the only thing that can do that is—the mind.

'The chair over there is in the wrong position and I want to move it'.

It is no longer What Is—it is *what I think* I would like it to be.

That is all that has happened—the thinking 'that should not be there'.

That thought, of itself has no power whatsoever.

It is only a thought, it is only based on words. But it refers to 'I' that I believe—or have believed myself to be—up until investigation.

That is so because what has added to that 'I'—that belief—has become the 'self centre' or the 'reference point'. Everything is evaluated from that reference point—and because it is closely associated with that pure intelligence—it has come to believe also that *it is* the intelligence.

Like the piece of iron in the fire—it will get red-hot and burn, just like fire.

Now if it had a mind it would think it was the fire. 'I am going to burn this and that'. But take it out of the fire and what can it do?

So it is with the thought—'I can—I will—I am'.

Take it away from awareness—or consciousness—or that pure intelligence—what substance has it got?

Can it stand without that?

Can you have a single thought—if you are not conscious or not aware?

Constantly over the years with the habit pattern going on—it has believed itself to be the intelligence—it believes it has reality—it has power, it has will—it can do what it likes and what it thinks it wants to do. That is why investigation is needed—just stop and question and have a look at what we have believed ourselves to be.

It can't of itself—do anything! Because that thought 'I see'—*can't see!* The thought 'I hear'—*can't hear!*

The thought 'I am aware'—*can't be aware!*

But—*there is* seeing—*there is* hearing and *there is* awareness.

It is happening right now!

The seeing itself cannot conceptualize, it cannot say 'I am seeing this'. Neither can the hearing say 'I am hearing this'—It is just pure seeing and pure hearing—it is conceptualized by the mind which must refer to some *past memory,* to get that name. So the mind or the 'me' that I have about myself—*is the past.* That is all it is.

It is the past and the past is dead—it is gone—it has happened. It is not *What Is.*

So that centre, that we constantly refer to, or believe in, is a dead image.

Now, can you understand why it can never be happy, can never be complete or whole—because it can't keep up with *What Is.* What Is—is this manifestation, this transient manifestation which is constantly changing.

Like the river, it is constantly flowing. How can a bucket of water taken from the river keep up with the river? It is impossible.

So, we tell you right here, that what you are seeking—*you already are!*

The idea of a separation is only a concept. With that idea of separation, there immediately comes along with it, the sense of insecurity—vulnerability.

Anything that thinks or believes it is separate—must also feel isolated and alone—apart from—other than me.

That is the way the mind functions—as soon as there

is 'me' there must be 'other than me' and that is the seeming separation—that is the cause of all of our problems.

When that is understood—what problem is there?— If there is no centre to refer it to.

Got it?

Q: The mind is just thinking that there is a problem.

Exactly, it is the nature of the mind to start stories and add to them and keep adding to them. You must see from that, that there can never be any answer in the mind. So, if there is no answer in the mind—what must happen? Whatever direction you go in, must be in the mind. So, full stop.

In seeing and being with that—even in that split second—to know that there is nothing wrong with right now—unless I am thinking about it—to know that, then after that, does it matter whether the mind is there or not?

Because, if the mind has been seen through and understood, it is not going to be given the same belief—just the same in the understanding that the blue sky is not really blue but we still see it as blue and acknowledge it when saying 'what a beautiful blue sky'. But we know the truth about it.

As the scripture says—'**know the truth and the truth will set you free**'.

Know the truth about yourself! You will see that you ever were free.

You were always free.

Just a seemingly erroneous belief, we ignore our true nature and believing the appearance.

Q: You have got to use the mind to reach this conclusion but the mind has such deep programming. The idea of intellectually knowing the truth, I find in practice, I can know it and I can try and stop the mind but basically it takes time for me to accept it gradually.

I can be told it, I can understand it, as a little bit more and a little bit more, it takes time.

As you say, we have got to use the mind. Well, the only instrument that we have is the mind. That is why the mind needs to be understood.

Understood thoroughly!

Then it is there as a very useful instrument.

You say that all this programming is there. Now understand—the mind is the past, it is the 'me', it is the conditioning—all this so called programming. Can the mind be rid of this past?

Q: I would have thought it was more about putting the mind in its place.

Yes but can it be rid of the past?

Q: No!

No, of course it can't. Because *it is* the past! So, when you see that, what would you do?

Q: Well, I would say you stand back from it.

Exactly, so what has happened to the past if you are not involved with it in the mind?

Q: Well, it is just a part of the mind.

72

So what has happened to your programming?

Q: It has gone.

Right! That's it, purely and simply.

Q: Yes but the technique would have to be constant.

See what you are doing is starting up a story, instead of staying with it and seeing it for yourself—in seeing it, you won't be worrying about technique. To have a technique means that you have to use the mind.

Q: The technique is to stay with it. To stop. But I call it a technique because I have got to say that I will make a decision that when ever I am aware that my mind is doing anything, that I will stop.
    Stop and say 'who am I?' or whatever.

It won't have to do even that! Afterwards. You know that the answer is not in the mind—that the mind is the past—you have stopped long enough to see that at one time or another. Then does it matter whether the programming goes on? What is the programming then? Who does it belong to? It is seemingly happening.
    Is it going to have the same intensity that it had before?

Q: The operative word for me is 'knowing' it. What I have found is that eventually they become my truth—'I know them' and there is no problem—I know them—but at the moment, this mind keeps going and I use techniques to control this mind, to the extent, in that I focus on things and do some work.

73

Who is the controller? If there is seemingly control going on ... *Who?*

Q: I would say that decisions are taken.

Of course decisions are taken. What is this 'I' that is saying it?

It is happening in this moment, it is happening presently. You are aware of that going on. Now, if that 'I' thought—can't see, can't be aware—has no power of its own—then when did it ever have it?

Q: Well it never did.

So, that means that all the seeming decisions you have made, all the activities that you have ever taken in your life, have not been *done by you*—as a separate entity. That is what has happened.

Q: Yes, I don't have a problem with that.

So, any control that has come up, anything that you have said that you have done has happened in spite of the 'you' being there. Anything you have thought, felt, tasted, touched or smelt is happening effortlessly just like your breathing is happening effortlessly—heart beating—hair growing—food digesting—All effortlessly without a 'personal doer'.

The thing is—that because *you believe*—and *have believed* for so long in personal doership—you take the personal responsibility.

Q: So, your saying that you walk down the street and you get to the corner and you don't know whether to turn right and go

*down and get a newspaper or go left and do something else—
and you stand at the corner and the mind says ' what will I do,
will I get the newspaper or will I go and have a cup of tea?*

*'I think I will get a newspaper'. Now as I see it, that
mind has done a job.*

Yes—it is there as an instrument to be used.

*Q: Even though there is no 'I' making decisions, the mind
still has to make decisions. So, the mind has to say 'do this,
that and so on, create this or that or don't'.*

The mind, when it sees that it has no power of its own—
it aligns itself with that intelligence—is a receiver for
what comes from that intelligence.

The problem arises because it translates that input
as this particular thought and 'I will do'—or 'I won't
do'—without it being put into the idea of a 'me', which
is past and has lost the spontaneity of the moment and
it is referring to yesterday—*without that*—it is
functioning directly and spontaneously from the
intelligence.

*Q: In our tradition it says that—'the spiritual path is
all inclusive, never exclusive'. It is an incredible
sentence. So everything that is possible for me to
experience—is it! I am a done deal because I have no
say in the matter.*

When it dawns on you—you realize 'Ah! I realize it'.
If it is One without a second—it is non dual—nothing
is exclusive.

Q: What I find is there is an incremental freedom—sections keep falling away. I know intellectually what you are saying—but as far as the lights going on, no—they just fall away bit by bit.

There is a wanting some experience—to be able to say 'this is it'.

Q: Is it possible to have a deeper understanding?

Who would have a deeper understanding?

Q: So, if it is not possible to have a deeper understanding, it is not possible for anyone to know what a dead mind would feel, sound or look like?

What is a dead mind—what mind is there? What is the mind? Apart from thought, is there any such thing? The mind *is the 'me'*—it is the ego—it is the past—it is all of those things. Seeing that—then it is dead right now. When that is understood what more is necessary? That is why Nisargadatta said 'Understanding is all'.

Q: I am dealing with people's trauma's all day, it is a constant contact with 'trauma' for about eight hours a day. After—I go home to a young family and experience the growing children. It is an incredible contrast. So, although, mostly I feel relaxed and detached from it all, I do find myself being swept away in all that. I still find myself feeling deflated or sorry for myself. I still suffer constantly.

Where would it be happening—what would it be happening to in those others that you see?

Q: Well, there are genuine physical symptoms but most of

it is in their minds.

So, it is being referred to that image that they have of themselves.

So that is the cause—and the effects that are coming up are from that.

But when you understand that image that you have, has no power, are you going to fall into the same old hypnotism, the same old conditioning?

Or—are you going to step away from it?

Q: I still fall into the trap of analyzing 'why' or 'where' is that coming from?

Get back to the basics—everything is registered right now, *just as it is.*

The only thing that can change *What Is*—alter it, modify it or correct it—is what comes up in the mind. Now—that content in the mind is also just registered just as is. What happens? You leave it there—you don't try and carry on trying to modify or correct that thought that has come up.

But this is what we do—'I don't like this' or 'I shouldn't be doing it' or 'I shouldn't be thinking'. It is still *as is*—**and what is wrong with *right now* unless you're thinking about it?**

What is wrong with right now, if we *are* thinking about it and not locking into the thought? Seeing the thought for what it is. Just *What Is* also!

Then it loses its sting.

But first see that it is that 'I' thought—that is the cause of the seeming separation—see that that is the cause of all our seeming problems.

It becomes the reference point which everything is

referred to—everything is relative to 'me'.

It is good, bad, pleasant, painful? According to what the 'me' thinks about it or what idea it has about it. See that the thought is not the real—then, how can you ever believe in it again?

The word itself is not the real—it is only 'pointing' at something.

Q: I know now what we are talking about but this mind has this perception that it is a prisoner—that it is separate and there is pain because of that—but intellectually—no.

It is a thought. On an emotional level I don't accept it.

What is the emotional level? What is the difference between the thought and the emotion?

Q: The mind creates the emotions.

Yes, so it is on the same level, you are not accepting it with the mind because—if you see clearly now—can that mind see? Can it be aware? Can it think?

Can that thought 'I see'—see?

Q: No, no.

Are you seeing right now?

Q: Yes.

Now, see that without that thought—seeing is happening, hearing is happening. Now—you don't need that *thought* to see—to be aware.

Q: I am allowing myself to have these thoughts to discuss

this with you but I am not troubled—because I don't allow them.

But see what I am getting at—if the 'I see' can't see and the 'I hear' can't hear—what do you attribute the intellectual level and the other level to?

Q: Yes, what is that? That is the One, there is no separateness.

Well, there can't be two levels. The intellectual level must be contributing to the 'I see' and the 'I hear'—as different from the pure seeing and the pure hearing. What is the primary truth that is with you right now?

Q: I suppose it is 'I am'

Yes, knowing that *you are!* 'Knowing that you are'. That is not some 'thing'!

That is just pure knowing. That is not intellectual.

There is no need for the mind for that! So, to know something—there is a concept in the mind.

You see, you are hearing those cars go by, you are seeing the colours in the room.

What is happening? There is an immediate 'knowing' of that.

You do not say 'that car is going by' while you are listening to me. It is registered and that means that there is a 'knowing-ness' of it.

That is not intellectual. That is the difference between thinking mind and that pure intelligence.

Very subtle split.

Can't you see—that there has to be the 'knowing' first! Then it is labeled by the mind.

Q: I do know it—but this mind says 'I don't know it'. This mind keeps creating its own reality.

But it can't—it has no power. If you see that, then you won't believe it any more.

Q: No, well I don't believe it.

If you don't believe it—if it is not believed in, would there be any energy going into it?

Q: No. I don't think so.

No, well then—it has come to a stop then. It can't live without energy.

The reason that it is going on is because you are still continually feeding it. You are believing that it has some power. You are not seeing that *of itself*—it can't do anything.

Q: Whenever I become aware of ...

That is involvement with the mind—there is no becoming—you are aware! Come back to the primary. Can you have a single thought without that awareness? That awareness is there already—can you *fall out of presence?*

Q: No.

No—so whatever is going on—is nothing other than *presence.*

But you are giving it the name and appearance and believing in the name and form—giving it that seeming reality by the belief in it. Belief becomes the reference point then.

Q: I don't have a problem with any of that—what I suppose that we are talking about here is the Ultimate Truth.

You are that! You have never moved away from that. Whatever appears on it is nothing other than it, appearing as different. Where can you go?

Q: Nowhere.

Right. So all those words you use—you haven't escaped from it.

Q: Yes, I think this word 'realized' is a good one, to become realized!

There is no becoming! What you are, you already are.

Q: I don't have a problem—this mind that is communicating with you, doesn't have a problem with all these concepts and this truth. But...

Never mind the 'but'—if you don't have a problem, then leave it at that.

Full stop—and *you are there!* See what I mean?

That is the subtleness of it, it *(the mind)* wants to create another 'story'.

If you're not creating another story, then you have got to be quiet. The last concept you have to drop is that 'Someday, I'm going to get it'.

What time is there?

Q: Yeah, Now!

81

Right....full stop!

Drop the concept of having 'some future time' that it is going to happen in and there is *no problem*.

Q: This 'who am I?' Is a beautiful thing, you don't get an answer, all I experience is those three words that are not a question. I am just one with those three words.

When you ask the question 'who am I?' You look for the source—or even where that question came from—can you point at that source?

Is there any particular spot in this body or in the so called mind where that question arose?

Q: No.

Any place it disappeared in?

Q: No.

So, what are you left with?

Q: Nothing!

No-thing—Not a thing. That is a *definite proof* that all this referral to a 'me' or a centre—has no particular place where it begins and no particular place where it ends.

Q: Yes, I agree, I see that there is no difference between the 'pre-state', where all the talking and thinking occurs on— and the state of just talking. There is no difference.

There couldn't be any difference, could there? Because

it is One—without a second—it is Omnipresence—it is All Presence.

That includes all the conversations—all the feelings—all the thoughts—all the manifestation, the whole lot. It is Omniscience—it is All Knowing—it is knowing the intellect—it is pure knowing.

Q: So, one is incapable of being deeper than another because of that. I sit and argue with these people that say there is a fathomless, bottomless depth of this thing that is 'before the talking'—and I just react to that. Then they say that—that reaction is a belief in a self-centre. What does that mean?

A belief is another reference point or a centre. Why do people get up in arms when you attack their beliefs?—Because it questions their centre.

That is what they are referring to. If they are a Christian or a Buddhist—and 'this is my belief'—they immediately get all up on end. Because that sense of seeming security is in that belief.

That is why I say that there does not matter if there is silence 'here'—and there can be long periods of silence—or it does not matter if the chatter is going on seemingly non stop—they are both experience.

They are both appearing on that pure 'knowing'.

The mirror will reflect the so called 'good thing' and the 'bad thing'—It doesn't make a scrap of difference what it is. *Just as it is.* So everything is reflected *just as it is.* Even the discriminating processes that come up with that—are still reflected *just as is.*

Q: So, the on going things like jobs and parents and children—that is just the on going energy and consequence and conditioning and all that...

If the focus is not in all that chatter that goes on about it—then it is going to appear effortlessly—it will fall into place, whichever way it goes.

Just like your breathing—your heart beating.

Q: So all this suffering comes from the competition—the jostling one-up-man-ship?

Well, have a look at it, as soon as that 'me' is there—that is the primary separation. The mind functions in the pairs of opposites—it cannot function in any other way. So, as soon as there is a 'me'—that implies that there is something 'other than me'. So, if I am not whole or complete, then immediate insecurity comes up. So all that jostling is trying to gather as much around itself as it can—to get as strong as it can—to seemingly protect itself.

But if you understand what the scriptures tell us—that it is One without a second—that omnipresence—omniscience that presence. *Everything is That.*

You have never moved away from it.

In that, 'knowing' that—there is total security.

Know that you are birth-less—death-less—time-less—space-less—body-less—mind-less and the happenings go on—but to whom?

Q: Yes, but the mind wants 'a win'.

Yes, but seeing that the answer is never in the mind—you know that you can't win—so—drop it! Why bother with it?

It will dawn on you. Just like when you walk out of the house and you get a mile down the road and it dawns on you that you have left the keys at home.

It will just dawn on you. Why did you leave your

keys at home? Just a little bit of inattentiveness to What Is, at the time. It will just dawn on you.

We have been conditioned to look 'out there' for it. We have been looking in the wrong direction—when you turn back and ask 'who am I'—and find that there is no 'me'—*the 'me'* can't see—can't hear—can't be aware—then—when were you ever separate?

The whole thing collapses. It collapses immediately—if there is no separation—where can I go? What can I do? Can I ever get away from it—can anyone ever fall out of presence?

Even when you say that 'I have forgotten'—when are you saying it? You're saying it presently! The very act of saying it—is presence.

Q: What about when the mind gets into the illusion, like fear and such?

You see—as soon as What Is, is named as fear— immediately there comes that belief of pain and there is an immediate movement trying to escape it.

If it just is *What Is*—do you have to move away from it?

You are seeing it fresh and new. Could it be fear?

Q: That is the hardest thing! Any kind of understanding is being an individual—but not being an individual, you are everything! You can't win ever, being an individual.

When you go to 'Who am I?' You can't find where that thought starts because there is no particular place where it starts—where it ends, you can not place it anywhere inside this body. So, it means it is everywhere and nowhere. So when it comes up after that, if that is seen, the mirage is still going to appear. But the next time you see it—you know it for what it is—you have seen through it—it is still there—it is still seemingly real—just like the blue sky, you will still acknowledge it by saying ' what a beautiful blue sky'—but you know full well that it isn't blue.

So the 'me' comes up, just like the actor on the stage—you're acting it out—things are happening.

But you know damn well that it is not what you are.

Nothing has changed—yet everything has changed.

Q: Well, what has been happening is this, when I hear you say that the answer is not in the mind, I see that the answer is in the present moment.

You have the answer immediately—a realization. If the answer is not in the mind—where else can it be?

It must be right here... right now... as What Is.

So, you know the answer—and that is **pure knowing.**

Q: Until that dawning happens, you're constantly bringing that intellectual understanding into the present and trying to get that imprisoned mind to experience the awakening. It is incredible that when we hear that the answer is not in the mind—that we don't just go there.

You can't go there and you can't get away either!

Q: But from the point of view of the mind—it is something that it wants to get.

It is right here—right now—as What Is. In knowing that—how can there be any conflict?

Relax and be what you are.

'It is the nature of the mind to start stories and add to them and keep adding to them. You must see from that, that there can never be any answer in the mind'.

೫

4

Presence Awareness

Q: *There is an idea that is currently common in the 'body work' modalities—that all of the tissues have some sort of memory. If you stimulate this part then there may come up some emotion or memories are triggered.*

Well, instead of going back or trying to look back at it—start from the source—what is it? It is all energy isn't it! Every cell is pure intelligence energy and in the space between the cells is pure intelligence energy. So that energy has to flow—the body is a pattern of energy and the mind also is a pattern of energy—they are nothing other than that.

The nature of the mind which is vibrating as this pattern of energy, it seems to divide everything into the pairs of opposites—good, bad—pleasure, pain—future, past or whatever and these thought patterns, what are they?

The energy in the mind is the same energy that is in the body—we say it is connected but it is one and the same thing.

A lot of the memories get locked in the body from the past—so the energy is blocked. So when there is a realizing or a seeing of some of these things, then that energy is released and it starts to flow again. So it might come out as thought patterns or memories or pain. You see it clearly and you think, well I've released that but it never really had any substance— it is just the energy that is seemingly blocked there and stagnated.

So when one is expanded and open, the energy is flowing there is no problem.

But if there is tension or a headache—what does one do?

Come back to the source and ask 'who is it happening to?' Thoughts are coming and going and the energy is vibrating right now—then there is nowhere in the head or the body where it can lodge.

But all this is a sense of belief—we give it some sense of reality—of realness—of concreteness and so our beliefs are a problem. If you haven't got that belief— you're not taking a stand anywhere—then there can be no seeming blockage can there? What the blockage is is energy resisting energy.

If I don't like this that is happening, then the resistance comes up trying to alter or modify What Is. Why do we try to alter or modify or correct What Is— because we believe we can do it better or 'it shouldn't be like this'. That is all based on our previous conditioning—if that wasn't there it would be as it is anyway, wouldn't it.

In one of the old Chinese scriptures it says 'In the mind—no mind—in the thought—no thought' Now a lot misinterpret that, it doesn't say don't have thought—what it means is to have the thought 'no mind' in the mind and the thought 'no thought' as a thought.

With that thought 'no thought' then the thoughts have no chance to take hold.

Benoit said 'when a thought appears, just step over it' then another thought will come but your not fixating on anything. They just come and go. Then there is no chance for any tension to lodge anywhere because it is not abiding anywhere.

We all say 'I am', that sense of presence that expresses through the mind as that thought 'I am'.

Now, that sense of presence, is it your sense of presence?

Is it my awareness of presence?

Or is it—just that sense of presence?

This pure present awareness. Just this.

There is nothing other than that. So, if you are seeking illumination, realization or oneness with God or what ever, then let it be *seen directly* that what you are seeking, you already are. You are already—and always have been.

You see, if you like to call it God—or what ever concepts you want to put on it—I prefer to call it— Intelligence Energy. A definition of God is Omni-potence, Omni-presence and Omni-science.

That means all power, all presence and all knowing. Now, where does that leave room for 'you' or for 'me'? Or anything other than that? So, any concept about *my God is better than your God* or my *Higher Power or Lower Power* is nonsense. Where is the room for 'you', if God is *all power and all presence?*

91

This is what we point out here directly. That there is just that One without a second. This intelligence energy is expressing itself effortlessly. Your only problem is when that sense of presence is expressed through the mind as the thought 'I am', the conditioning has been added to that thought 'I am' and formed an image.

At about the age of two years, reasoning has started to happen to you—along with the events and experiences and this has formed an image which we call 'me'. It is *an idea,* a thought in the mind.

Now, being mechanical, the mind can only function in the inter-related opposites, this thought 'I am' is what has caused our *seeming separation.* It is the primary dualism. *('I'—'not I' 'self'—'other')*

As soon as there is an 'I'— there must be a 'you' or a 'this' or 'that' as opposed to 'I' and so with that 'I' and 'you' there is an immediate sense of separation— An immediate sense of fragmentation, which is, isolation and loneliness, fear and insecurity.

If I believe that I am separate, then quite naturally, there is that insecurity there.

There is that *seeming* sense of isolation and fragmentation.

From then on our life is geared to becoming whole, happy, complete. Because the conditioning is *'to look out there',* we seek it 'Out there'.

As it was said earlier, first off, we seek a secure, loving family around us. The next level is the tribe. Then the next is the National. Nations go to war with nations to try to protect that sense of insecurity, that vulnerability which we all have.

We are frightened that something or someone will take something from us.

We have to add and accumulate as much as we can to make us more secure.

We are told that if we get a good education, a good job, make more money—have a bigger car, a bigger house or form a good relationship— all these things will give us that happiness and security that we have been seeking.

When you come here, stop and question, have a look at what you believe yourself to be. Just have a look at this *seeming* centre, this reference point, which I refer to as 'I' or 'me'.

What is it? Where does it start?

What is it composed of?

Where is the centre that I believe to be me?

Is it in this body anywhere? Is it in this mind?

As soon as this questioning starts along these lines, things are bound to happen.

Because the false cannot stand up to investigation.

What we believed without question all our lives cannot stand up to it.

It falls apart. That 'I' thought has no substance of its own, it cannot stand on its own. It needs that pure intelligence or consciousness or awareness behind it before you can have a single thought.

Whatever you like to call it.

There is nobody here now, or at any other time, that can negate their Being-ness. No one can ever say 'I am not'.

That knowingness is what intelligence is, that activity of knowing, that knowingness is constantly there.

It is prior to the thought 'I am'.

There is no need to repeat I am, I am, I am.

That being-ness expresses itself through the thought

'I am'. Whether you are saying it or not, there is still that knowing that you are.

That *Being-ness* or *Living-ness*.

That intelligence energy is expressing itself effortlessly.

Last Thursday I asked those present, to define 'Living'.

So, now, can you define for me 'Living'?

An answer—'a succession of . . . err . . Happenings'...

That is *an expression* of living.   What is Living?

Another answer. 'Breathing'.

That too is *an expression* of Living.

Another answer ...*'There is no word for it, this is it!'*

See, it is just like the wind, can you show me the wind?

All you can see about the wind, is *an expression* of it. It is waving the flag. It is moving the grass. It is moving the branches of the trees—or what ever it is moving.

Well, this Living-ness, you can not define it! —Why? Tell me why?

'You can't see it'.   Can't feel it'

Why?

'Because you are separate from it when you try to name it'—You are that!

You are that Living-ness!

So the Livingness cannot be defined, because you are that. All that can be defined is what appears in it and on that Livingness. In other words, some expression of it.

So that pure Being-ness or Living-ness is what you are.

You are that Living-ness!

Just like the eye cannot see itself. You can *never* grasp it with the mind.

Without that Living-ness, could anyone have a single thought?

It contains the thinking. The thinking cannot contain it.

This beingness, this sense of presence—it hasn't changed—from the time I can first remember—looking back from here, I know it was the same sense of presence—of 'I am' when I was a little child.

That sense of presence has not changed—it is untouched.

It can never be touched.

Not touched by time. It has not grown older or younger. Why?

Because it contains time. It is not touched by space. Why?

Because it contains space.

That is why it says in the '*Gita*.'

'*The sword can't cut it, the fire can't burn it, the wind can't dry it and the water can't drown it*'. Why?

Because, it contains all of this manifestation.

There is no 'Thing' that can contain 'It' or grasp 'It'.

You see, we see all the objects in this room here but we never take notice of the space.

If it was not for the space—the volume, there would not be any room for the objects. Space is always there before the objects. To the mind—the objects are more attractive than the space.

The space is no-thing. It is the same with awareness, there could not be a single thought if you were not conscious or aware.

So if we know that the answers not in the mind, what might happen?

An answer 'We stop looking there'.

Yes, we can stop looking there.

How many years have you been searching for the answer?

How many years did we try to work it all out?

The answers to life or livingness itself, you've never found because it's not something you can grasp, tuck it away in some mental corner and go on living.

We see that all that this *self centre* is, is an image, or an idea in the mind, of a self that's got no substance.

The answer is not in the mind. Can you seek in any other place than the mind?

We can use the analogy of *'the iron in the fire'*.

We put the iron in the fire.

It will become red like the fire. It will become hot like the fire. If you grasp it, it will burn you like the fire.

It takes on the attributes of the fire.

Now, take it out of the fire, what will it do? Will it get red?

Will it burn?

It has no substance of its own. It has nowhere to stand and no power to do these things—to be red hot, to burn.

It has no *power of its own* to do these things.

So—the same with this idea that I have about myself.

If it wasn't for that pure intelligence in the background, I couldn't have a single thought.

It can't stand on its own. Another way of putting it is—each one of you is seeing right now—you are hearing right now. Is that so?

Tell me, does the ear say 'I hear'?

Or does the eye say 'I see'?
Does the backside sitting on the seat say 'I feel'?
(Silence)
Well, does it?

'*No*' (general agreement)

What says, I see, I hear, I feel?
Doesn't a thought come up translating what is happening as I see or I hear?
Look at it from another angle, does the '*idea*' in the mind 'I see'—see?
Does the idea in the mind '*I hear*' hear?
Or does the idea in the mind '*I feel*', does that feel?

'*No*'

The thought comes up *after* the seeing, *after* the hearing.
It is all happening prior to the thinking, just as it is.
So you can see from that, it's like the piece of iron.
It has taken on the attributes of that pure intelligence, which is registering everything AS IT IS— and believes *itself* to have the power.
You can see from that, added to this image of myself, it believes it has personal volition, has personal power.
In addition—It needs a God or something else to make it whole because things are not going the way it expects it to. If it had such power—why are things not going the way it wants it to?
If it is running the show!
The unlimited potential has limited itself into the shape or form of a poor miserable human being—and we live from that point until we see that we were never that.

All these pointers you will see when you start to question.

You will see clearly that this idea or image that I have about myself is not what I really am at all.

It is an idea based on past events and experiences.

Not only does it have no reality as such but it's a *dead image*.

It is based on yesterday—yesterday's events and happenings.

There is no livingness in it whatsoever. As it appears and comes up, it comes up presently—like the piece of iron in the fire—it is in the fire and heated by the fire—and so it is with the intelligence, the intelligence is heating up this idea, this image and it believes itself to have the power.

But it never did have!

In seeing that, *'there is no centre here'*, then I'm free from that *seeming* bondage.

The cage that I have built around myself—*the cage of limitations*, is that I believe myself to be a separate entity, a person, an individual.

As soon as that idea of separation comes, there is immediate insecurity—immediate vulnerability and the anxieties, fears, resentments, self-pity and everything else must come from that image of separation, because it is trying to make itself whole or complete.

You are the timeless!

Thought is time—appearing on the timeless.

Well, look from the other way, right here, right now, everyone is breathing, everyone's heart is beating, blood is coursing around the body.

Hair is growing, finger nails are growing. Cells are being replaced, food is being digested. Who is making any effort to do it?

Is there any 'me' or idea in the mind saying, 'I have to take the next breath'?

'I've got to beat my heart. I have to digest my food', or is it happening—effortlessly?

Is there an innate intrinsic intelligence, an energy within that manifestation of the body that is coursing the blood through your veins right now?

Causing the diaphragm to draw down, bringing in the air, then pushing it up to expel the air. It is taking all the food and all these various things that are needed to these different cells. You can feel that energy, you can feel it in your finger tips and in your toes, if you like to watch closely enough.

To feel closely enough—You can feel it there, pulsating, throbbing.

The Livingness pulsing and throbbing through this pattern of energy right now.

Effortlessly. No one making an effort to do it.

It is even causing the thinking. That energy has to find outlets.

It shines out of your eyes as light by which you see the world.

What effort are you making to 'see'?

What effort are you making for that light to be in your eyes?

What effort to hear?

That intelligence—that innate intrinsic intelligence, which pulsates through this body, is registering everything, right here, right now, just as it is.

Direct experience of this—right now.

Just like a mirror reflects everything just as it is.

Or a camera takes a photograph—just as it is.

You are hearing the cars going by—You are seeing

the movements in this room.

Smelling any odors that are present.

All registered just as it is and I mean—*Just As It Is.*

It is un-corrected, un-modified, unaltered, just purely and simply, as is.

The mind names things.

There are gaps in the thoughts continually where it is starting and stopping—within you.

Seeing and knowing that—those gaps become longer.

The seeing and the hearing, can and do happen without the *'naming'*.

Just being registered 'as is'.

It is not the nature of the mind to be simple.

It will go on analyzing—analysis paralysis—creating all sorts of stories just to perpetuate itself.

The mind will come up and try to modify what is, try and correct it or alter it. 'I don't like this'—'this is good'—'this is bad'. Then there is—a *resistance* to What Is.

The mind is translating what is being registered.

You don't have to look very hard to see that—any resistance is conflict.

So, the idea that I don't like this is just an idea in the mind.

What is it that I don't like? I don't like the chair or the table.

How do I 'know' that it's a chair or a table?

I have *named it* from some previous experience.

I'm no longer with What Is.

I'm with *the 'name'*.

So the name I've given it is just another idea in the mind, so the mind is in conflict with itself, a seeming energy blockage, a resistance to What Is.

If it is just what is and there is no resistance to it, what is happening?

There's no conflict there whatsoever and things just express as is. That doesn't mean you have to sit down and do something.

Everything will be done, as is.

But if the resistance comes up and 'I don't like this'— then what happens?

That thought gets hold of it and builds it up and builds it up and builds it up.

So what starts off as a little resentment will build up until the energy will be such that it has to be acted on.

It will come out as some activity, anger, violence or whatever.

So you see, this is where all 'my' problems arise from, that dualism, me and the other.

That sense of separation - that insecurity—that 'me' fears the unknown.

Because that 'Me'—*IS* the separation—it constantly fears.

So it would rather stay in the old way, no matter how unpleasant it is. 'I'll stay here rather than step out into the unknown'. Take that step into the unknown—into the 'no thing' and see. An old saying is—**Do the thing you fear and the death of fear is certain.**

Let the intuitive take over without the 'me' thinking it knows better.

So, I understand there is no *'me'*, from this point of view, it has been seen clearly. Then I also understand that there can be no *'you'*, as such either.

So, if there is no 'me' and there is no 'you', who is superior?

Or who is inferior? What would I want of yours?

In the East, cause and effect is called *Karma* and in the Christian religion 'As ye sow, so shall ye reap'.

Remove the cause and what must happen to the effect?

The effect must drop off also. There cannot be an effect without a cause.

And that is all that simply has to happen.

Without the mind, without the thinking—right now—snap off the thinking for just a moment or just keep the mind full by saying 'no mind—no thought'—'no mind—no thought'.

Any thought other than that—just say 'no thought'.

While you were doing this, did you stop hearing, breathing, feeling or seeing?

Realize from that, that everything was still being registered while the mind was occupied with the thought 'no thought'.

That is another proof that you are not the mind.

See, the cause of all my problems is 'me', this self centre.

This image that everything is relative to. This dead image, it is not the livingness.

It is based on 'yesterday'. Then if the image is not there, then the livingness must be there in its fullness.

Don't you know that this intelligence has brought me right here and right now?

Through all the dramas and traumas and things that happen, it has brought me through that, don't you know that it is going to continue?

...continue to look after this body-mind, this pattern

of energy, for as long as the body-mind is going to be around.

In this, without that effort, isn't there a great sense of freedom?

Just the freedom—To Be—Which I am anyway.

'What you are seeking you already are! So it is foolish to carry on the search. The only place the search started from is in the mind'.

ॐ

5

Be what you are

The cage of self-centeredness which I build around myself, a cage of words, is a phantom. It does not exist!

The cage door is open right now. As a matter of fact, the whole cage can be seen to be what it is and will fall away. Right now.

The cage of limitations. Words. Good, bad, pleasant, painful, positive, negative, possible, impossible. All words.

The word is not the real. You can say water, water for the rest of your life. Try and drink the word!

The word is a symbol for something else. It is not the real.

And yet when I say, 'I'm no good' or 'I have low self esteem'

What reality has it got?

Or look at it the other way, 'I'm superior, I'm better'.

Is that what you are?

What does that symbolize?

Can it be there at all if there is no living-ness?

Instead of trying to come up with an answer in the mind, wouldn't it be wise to just be with this living-ness?

To be with this being-ness, to settle down with this presence.

Watch how it is expressing. Feel it shining through your eyes.

Lighting up your face. Feeling the breath.

Seeing it as it is.

Marveling at the very fact of 'seeing'.

All the variety and diversity that it can express there.

Marveling at all the different feelings that can come up in this way.

Instead of attaching to them and allowing them to build up until they get out of all proportion, until they have taken over exclusively, the whole of that awareness and functioning—like a cloud covering the sun, to the exclusion of everything else. We are seemingly lost in it.

When you stop stirring the water in the bucket, it becomes still.

It doesn't matter what your story is—'I should not have said that' or 'I should not have done such and such'—you're stirring the water!

Full stop! Right here—right now.

Even while the thinking is going on, I can be seemingly deeply absorbed in it all. Realize that there is still the sensation of sitting. There is still the hearing of the cars going by and whatever else is being heard.

There is still the tasting and the smelling.

Bring it back into its proper proportion. What room

106

is there for any problems? Problems are seen as they arise.

The activity takes place as necessary.

Then what is the problem? I can ask anyone of you right now: **What is wrong with right now unless you think about it?**

There is an instant pause, while you try and look to see what is wrong.

Realize that before anything can be wrong, there has to be thought.

So you see—come back to that constantly, right here, right now, presently, there is nothing wrong.

Just the same as, what past is there? Unless I think about it.

What future is there?—unless I think about it.

I hear some say that they can't stand to stay in the 'Right Now'—'I can't stand it!' When do you ever leave right now? When is it ever not present?

Only the mind again, creates an image, an image of yesterday or imagines and anticipates a tomorrow.

Time is a mental concept.

Now we are back where we started. Right here, right now, there is no one that is not present and aware of that presence. Is that so?

> 'Yes!' (general agreement)

Are there any questions?

Question: 'The mind is there, it operates, we don't have an alternative, so what is the answer?'

The mind is a wonderful instrument when it is

used rightly.

All the Art, the Technology and all the Creativity, it all comes through that mind.

Nisargadatta said 'The mind is a good servant but a bad master'

Q: 'So do we have to be taught how to utilize it? '

No, just coming back, realizing, presence. In this presence, everything is registering just as it is. Watching from that awareness you will recognize when the mind begins to go into the past or the future and that is—the head trip—It's trying to alter What Is. It is altering or modifying What Is and that is resistance.

There will be recognition of your resistance to things and that recognition must be from the point of *No resistance.*

We just need to recognize that this is resistance or in-attention.

In-attention is recognized from the point of attention. There is no one to be attentive, just notice that there is a little resistance or a little bit of inattention there.

In the moment of recognition, there is a subtle relaxation. From that moment, you are back in the moment with **What Is**.

Sooner or later, the recognition will come up again because now you are aware of it. Where before it was just ignored totally and not even thought about.

Now that it has been pointed out that there is no centre there, that there is no other time than presence.

The intelligence sees this and it sees when you are taken out of it.

'You are that pure intelligence, what can be added to you? Nothing! What can be taken away? Nothing!'

ॐ

Q: 'Do you meditate?'

Attention to What Is—*is meditation.* Sometimes I sit, sometimes I don't. There are long periods of silence here at times. And there will be periods of chatter but the both of them are experiences of the mind.

I can only say that I have a silent mind or a chattering mind through experiencing it.

What I am is prior to that—so it does not matter to me.

I don't prefer one over the other.

It does not make a difference, they are both—What 1s.

Q: 'Where does action come in?'

Action is spontaneous, it comes in, in the presence.

Q: 'You don't try to regulate it, you don't try and direct it?'

No, not at all. There is no one to direct it. It will be directed if that is what is necessary in the moment.

Q: 'So it's a totally passive concept then?'

Who is to be passive?

To say 'I'm going to be passive', you are back in that self centre.

It is to be alert with 'What Is' and that means you are totally with that activity of knowing and being.

More so than you've ever been before. It is just like living with a snake in the room.

You're going to watch its every move! You have no room for the head stuff. You'll be looking around taking in everything else that's going on.

The head stuff takes its proper place. Each of the senses is allotted a proper segment. But most of us are so used to being in the head—it has taken over the largest proportion and the other senses get a little bit.

But if everything is in its proper sequence, what's going to be a problem about this? What is seen from a narrow viewpoint in the 'me', when seen from the Totality, is something that can be handled, probably quite easily.

And what will happen? Nobody knows!

Once the old habit patterns are seen, once you have seen that it is all habit patterns, it can never get the same intensity that it had before.

The old habit patterns will continue for awhile—because they have been there for years and years as conditioned responses.

But once they have lost their hold and the energy has gone out of them. They are not going to stay.

There is no point in them.

Q: 'So we just watch the thoughts, Bob?'

You are *prior* to the thought. You are not the thought.

Be aware of it. In that registering, in that pure intelligence, it is all being witnessed just as it is.

As soon as there is some modification or correction, that is a thought. Now that is also just as it is.

The next thought will be just as it is. The next movement—just as it is.

Q: 'How does this concept fit with planning, is there no need for planning?'

If that comes up right now, plan, set it up, do what you

have to do now.

But instead of carrying it around in your head, mulling over it, 'What will be the outcome'—etc, etc. When the planned time becomes the present, act on it then. Carrying It around, it is weighing you down— etc... Planning is part of living, just the same as the memory is there to be used.

But when memory starts to use us, it becomes— self destructive!

Memory is a very necessary thing.

The mind *is not* the enemy!

But if you look at it in a different light and see, all the mind is, is a movement of energy, just the same as the whole manifestation.

This manifestation is pure intelligence energy, vibrating into different patterns—different shapes— different forms. It is like the sun light hitting the crystal.

The light comes out as those colours but what are those colours? Are they anything other than the sun's rays?

So this pure awareness is dancing around there as you, and here as Bob, and somebody else over there.

Has it changed its true nature?

After some time the crystal is moved or the sun's rays stop touching it. What happens? The rays are not shining through that particular form, have they been lost?

Q: 'This is interesting!'.

The real interest is to come back to—awareness presence—as quickly as possible.

Its essence—its true nature is that pure intelligence energy. It can never be added to or taken away from.

It is the changeless reality. So, we see that thinking patterns are energy.

If the energy doesn't go into it, they drop off.

Nothing gained, nothing lost, just What Is.

Q: *'It's amazing how easy it is to make a decision without all that clutter going on'.*

Well, it's easy enough for a decision to come up isn't it?

But then the clutter starts up again as to whether I have made the right decision. *(Laughter)*

What is word? Word is sound. What is thought? Thought is subtle sound. Sound is vibration. Vibration is energy.

The way it vibrates is in opposites, good-bad, pleasant-painful, past-future, positive-negative. All words!

Whatever comes through that pure intelligence, because *it is* the reality, it cannot change.

The definition of reality is: that which does not change.

It's just like the mirror. A mirror will reflect everything in it but no image in the mirror contaminates it.

So that pure intelligence is not contaminated by any thought or feeling.

When the mind realizes that it has no power, of itself, just like the piece of iron in the fire, then it aligns itself with that intelligence.

It's the vehicle through which that expression comes, which must be put into words, ideas, plans or whatever.

In other words, it is there for its proper function.

Q: *'This is where I have a problem, with planning and*

predicting a certain outcome'.

With the idea of 'doing' comes the 'me' that's going to 'do' something about it.
It starts up that self centeredness again.
There was never any 'me' there in the first place. All that is done is done from that functioning.

Q: *'Wasn't there a 'me' to select the outcome?'*

Not really, have a look and see what the 'me' is.
See for yourself that there never was a 'me'. The 'me' is only an idea in your mind.
If it has no substantiality, where is the bondage?
Where is the self centre? It is only the 'me' that is the cause of my problems.
If I am not functioning from that false centre, then I must be with What Is.

Q: *'Hard to accept in the first ten minutes'*.
(Everyone laughs and agrees)

We have years and years of habitually looking 'out there'*(Outside oneself)* ignoring our true nature.
Our problem is ignorance.
We ignore our true nature and go with what we are told.
'Johnny, you're a good little boy' or 'you're a bad little boy', you are this, that and the other and add to that all the events and experiences that happen and all this builds an image. This image is constantly changing.
Little bits being added to it, little bits taken away and something is always affecting this image. We didn't ever stop to look.

Once you have seen it clearly—as Christ said:
'Know the truth and the truth will set you free'.
This true investigation—sitting with it—and seeing the false as false—the image is then understood. It has no power of its own. It is known for certain.
It is not a belief.

Q: *'Was primitive man more in touch with it?'*

Not necessarily so. There would be those who were in touch with it as there always have been. Whatever direction you go in from this presence, this 'now', must be in the mind, in the thought.
If there is no thinking, what is wrong with 'right now'?
Is there any other thing than Right Now—if there is no thinking?
It is always presence.

Q: *'For a period of time, my life has been going well, in comparison to what it was before. However, sometimes my mind will tell me I need something to happen, to see how well I am. Why is that? Why, when things are going well, do I want to question things?'*

Here is a little story. There is this traveler in the desert. It's very, very hot and he is thirsty. In the distance there is one lone tree.
He didn't know that it was a 'Wish fulfilling Tree'.
He goes and sits beneath it and he thinks, 'This is nice,
I only wish I had a cool drink now'.
Low and behold—a cool drink appears in his hand.
'Oh! Terrific!' he says. 'Now if I had a soft bed to

lie on and drink this with a bit of a breeze to fan me.' Low and behold, a soft bed appeared as well as a maiden with fan, fanning him. 'Oh! This is terrific. Now all I need is a good meal to go with all this and everything would be just right'. Low and behold, a big meal appeared.

Then the mind said 'Hey! What's all this? What's going on? Maybe it's a devil?' And—the Devil appeared. The mind then says 'Oh! He's going to eat me'—and he does!

So, when everything is going right, the mind, just on its own, wants to question. This is the usual pattern. The answer is not in the mind, *full stop!*

If you understand that, what direction can you take from that?

Q: 'No direction'.

That's right, full stop. Any direction you take must be in the mind. Everything is being registered just as it is.

All the impressions are coming in through the senses, being registered, just as is.

The things that you have no vested interest in are of no concern what so ever.

If you got up and walked out of the room right now, you would step over those cushions. You wouldn't kick them out of the way.

You would step over them quite naturally. That means that it is all being registered without you thinking about it.

Realizing that that intelligence is functioning, that's the 'Razor's Edge'.

That is functioning.

The mind comes in and wants to discriminate,

modify it or alter it or correct it in some form or another.

So, you can rely on that pure intelligence which is effortlessly functioning in that body right now.

There is no centre here.

You must see the falseness of it.

You must see that it has no power of its own.

And this can happen only by looking—by investigating.

Stay with the awareness.

Let what *that essence is*—reveal itself to you—without that 'me' being in the way.

There is *Livingness* There is *Beingness*.

There is Awareness of that *being present*.

Just as it is.

This is what we call, *effortless living*.

You are being 'lived' effortlessly.

Nobody tells the stomach to digest the food.

Q: *'Even the awareness, it just is, that attentive-ness, it just is?'*

Yes!

Q: *'Bob, is this like a surrendering?'*

Well, have a look George and see—what is it that needs to surrender?

Q: *'I suppose we surrender the ego'*

Have a look at that, is there such a thing?

Q: *'No, there is not'.*

Well, how can you surrender something that is not

117

there? When you see that it is false and that it never existed, you don't have to surrender.

Full Stop. See that clearly!

Q: *'I try to bring myself in, in my mind and it's a struggle'.*

Let it go!

Q: *'Is it because it is unseen that we try to label it?'*

Yes, the mind has to try and grasp something.

It tries to give it a concept, an image. This it cannot grasp. So it will create all sorts of things.

It will even create a next life. At some future time, if I have been a *good boy that* has created a *God* and a *Heaven,* I'll go up there. (*Pointing upwards*)

Or—if it's in the East, I'll come back, I'll Reincarnate.

It's always *Becoming*—Instead of *Being*.

Becoming is some projected future time when things will be. There is *no future time to become in.*

But the actuality is *Right Now. This* is the *Living-ness.* You can never live this moment again.

This moment, right now.

Q: *'Where does the energy go when we die?'*

Where does a wave go when it drops back into the ocean?

Q: *'I don't know'*

Will that same wave come out again? *No*

Q: *'Where does the energy come from?'*

118

(Tapping his lower chest)
This is called the 'Solar Plexus', why?

The ancients called it the sun plexus. That is where this energy radiates out just like the sun radiates and gives life to the Earth.

This solar plexus is not contained in the body.

It animates the body. It is the life. It lives the body.

The Sun is the very life. It's the energy, the light, the heat, without it there would not be anything.

Energy comes into the body through the breath and goes out through the breath.

This energy goes all through the body to the ends of your toes and fingers.

It also radiates out to all those around you.

You are not the body, you are not the mind.

So what is the body?

Now when that sperm and ovum meet, that consciousness, that Living-ness, that cell doubles and re-doubles.

That little embryo starts to expand and the energy in it starts to spread and grow in the mother.

The heart starts beating before the brain is even formed.

So how can there be any 'I' for it there? It attunes itself to that warmth, the heartbeat and the breathing of the mother.
It is growing itself effortlessly.

So again, this is proof that this 'I' thought, this idea or image, of itself, has no power whatsoever.

It is powerless. That is not what I am.

Realize that this is what is happening.

You are being lived. That livingness itself.

Q: *'Nothing can happen to a 'non-me', everything just happens because I'm not a 'me'.*

Live from that point of view and see.

You will then start to see some of the scriptural statements start to come true.

'A thousand shall fall at thy side and ten thousand at thy right hand; but it shall not come nigh thy dwelling place '

I see this constantly—the world is still going on but there is very little comes here. What can come here is handled, simply, easily and effortlessly. Where before— I can remember a few years back, when I was involved in the whole bloody lot and it was destroying me.

But if you are that pure intelligence, what can be added to you?

Nothing!

What can be taken away?

Nothing!

When you are hungry, doesn't something let you know?

When you need to go to the toilet, doesn't something let you know?

This, so called, individual, innately and intrinsically knows it already.

But in its own mind it can't grasp it, so, it creates an image out there, which it has to 'hear it' *(the knowledge)* from.

All problems are problems of relationship.

'Me' and the 'other '.

If there is no relationship, what might happen?

A so called energy level or wave length will be attracted to you as is necessary in the pattern of energies.

Just like the bees are attracted to the flower, to pollinate, to express and recreate and rebuild this life.

There is only Life, only life.

There is no death. Life lives on life. When this so called body breaks down there is still life going on.

Because enzymes, microbes begin to change the pattern.

If the body is burnt it is reduced to ashes and they go back into the elements where it came from—what is lost?

The expression, the appearance or pattern is changed.

Is that intelligence that that energy is—is that lost? Knowing that—is there anything to fear?

Q: *'What is this fear that I feel?'*

If you look at it fresh and new without naming it, is it then fear?

You see, as soon as you say it's fear, you're naming it from the past.

The natural thing to do as we have always done is to try to avoid fear. The mind shuts off and tries to move away from it. It tries to create something else, instead of being with *What Is*.

So you are trying to alter or modify 'What Is' in some way. If you look at it—stay with it—going through it—see exactly what it is, see how it is then.

Q: *'There is nothing to need'.*

Needs are taken care of as necessary for the *functioning*.

Q: 'You have a lot better use of the energy'.

Yes—if that energy is not going on in the so called personal chatter, then it is there to be utilized in the moment, expressing it.

That thought 'I am' is in the mind.

That thought is what was born and that is what dies.

The mind wants to perpetuate itself. The mind is a wonderful instrument. It is not the enemy.

It doesn't have to be forcefully shut out or closed.

Q: 'What is desire?'

Desire is the fixation of the mind on an idea. Get out of its groove by denying it attention. The seeming 'doer' goes on until you see that there is no doer.

Q: 'It is the nature of the mind to perpetuate its own identity'.

Yes.

Q: 'By doing that it says 'well, if what you say is correct, that the mind doesn't have a separate identity'—the mind therefore has to deny what you're saying. So when the body passes and the mind passes, there is death'.

Yes, that thought 'I am' is what was born and that is what dies.

In St. Francis' prayer it says *'For it is only by dying that I can have Eternal life'.*

`He was not talking about the physical death. It is about dying to that sense of self, that 'me'.

St. Paul said *'I die daily'*. It is dying to that idea of mind. It just has to be understood.

Nisargadatta says 'Understanding is all'.

As children we have put upon us the idea of an ideal person. It's generally Christ or Buddha or one of the others.

Those who put this idea onto us, can't live up to it themselves. We get the idea that I should be like this or I shouldn't be like that and that is added to this image that we have about ourselves.

This image of an ideal person leads to the feeling 'I'm not good enough' or 'my self esteem is low'.

This is one of the greatest causes of our problems.

It has been imposed on us by others who never lived up to it either. Each one of us is intelligence expressing itself—each one is a unique expression.

No two expressions are the same. In all of the diversity within this cosmos or the manifestation of the universe, each point of expression is unique.

So a thought of how I should be, becomes a limiting factor-when you are that unique expression.

Stop pretending to be what you are not—be what you are! Just be! So relax—be open—be open in the heart.

It resonates—it is recognized—it is known—it is pure, simple, understanding.

Q: 'Is there more than one 'I'?'

There is not even one 'I'.

Q: 'But I mean 'to the mind', because there seems to be multiple'.

Where is that appearing? In the mind!

But then the mind will say 'I don't like this' (*what*

ever this is at any particular time.)

So, you see this 'I don't like this'—becomes a reference point.

So this reference point jumps in and creates another reference point, trying to escape the first reference point. So that's where the feeling comes up that there is more than one 'I'.

So, the mind will swap reference points continually.

This is the nature of the mind. Investigate and find that there is no particular point where you can say that this is where it all started. By continuously seeing the mind, it looses its power, its intensity.

Then it is there for what it is meant to be there for.

Break that habit pattern of 'Oh but' and 'If' and 'I know from past experience'.

That is what comes in through the mind and we lose our spontaneity and the intuitiveness.

The sixth sense is sometimes called the spiritual sense.

It will come up spontaneously but the mind will say—'oh no I've got something better'.

Q: *'Where does the duality start?'*

The habit pattern or that belief that—I am the doer!

Q: *'I don't have the courage to accept that I am not controlling my life'.*

See the limitation you place on it.

What is intelligence and energy? Isn't it courage itself? Isn't it love itself, compassion itself? You have all the courage you need.

But we put the limitation on it 'I don't have the

courage' etc...

Once it is seen clearly that there is no 'centre' here, even if you get caught in the habit patterns again—you only seemingly have lost it.

In the Knowing and the deep underlying reality of Knowing—this is never lost.

There is no beginning to it.
There is no ending to it.
Is there any separation?
Are you separate from the air you breath?
Are you separate from the earth you stand on?
What is this separation?
Is it just another concept?

> 'The mind, when it sees that it has no power of its own—it aligns itself with that intelligence—is a receiver for what comes from that intelligence'.

ॐ

6

The mind cannot change the mind

Q: Bob, what is the nature of your teaching?

This teaching embraces Advaita Vedanta, it embraces Kashmir Shaivism, it embraces Dzogchen—the highest form of Buddhism and it embraces the highest form of Christianity too. It is just that Non Duality, the One without a second or as it is said in Christian religion, Omniscience, Omnipotence, and Omnipresence—there is nothing other than That.

If there is nothing other than that, who is the Guru and who is the disciple? It is all That. We know this in our language, for instance, that is a chair, that is a cup, that is John—take the words chair, cup and John away and what is it? It is all That. There is nothing other than That. I am That—Thou art That—That Is That.

Q: What about the word GOD, are you comfortable with IT?

That all depends on the concept. You see the word

God has a lot of different concepts for a lot of different people. With some it is Christ and with others it is Buddha and with others it is something else. If God is Omniscience, Omnipotence and Omnipresence that is All Knowing—All Being and All Presence. I don't like to use that term because the recipient aligns it with their image or a definition, so I prefer to call it Intelligence Energy.

We are told that we are a 'person'—that we are a separate individual or a separate entity and naturally it is believed from then on. When you are a little child before the reasoning starts it is not 'I' do this or that', it is 'Johnny does this or Johnny wants that' whatever the name may be. Johnny does not see himself as a separate entity—then after awhile it becomes 'I'.

The thinking process seemingly forms the individual. With the registration of everything, everything is *just as it is*. All the thinking, the seeing, the hearing, the smelling, tasting and touch sensations are registered in the immediacy of this moment. But then as soon as the thought 'I' see' or 'I' hear' or 'I' think' comes up, who does it refer to? You see that 'I' in its purity cannot refer to anything—so added to it with that thinking process, is the image you have from your conditioning and from memory. That image is what you believe yourself to be. As soon as you say 'I am John or Bob' or whatever your name is, there immediately comes in the associated conditioning 'I am good' or 'I am bad' or 'I am special' or whatever the conditioning is.

'I am happy' or 'I am unhappy' or 'I am a doctor' or 'I am only a laborer and I'll never get anywhere in life'—whatever your belief or whatever the conditioning is that has happened in your life. Now that 'I' thought is the separating factor. The way the mind functions is only in the pairs of opposites. So as soon as that 'I' comes up there has to arise a 'you' or the 'other'—other than 'I'.

The very idea of that 'I' thought immediately implies separation—it implies isolation. That is vulnerability—that is fear.

Q: How do you see through this appearance of six billion separate individuals?

By investigation, by trying to find out in the first place, who is this 'I', who is this 'me'? Is it what I think I am? Is it what I believe myself to be?

What is that 'I' thought? Stay with it—to the mind it is 'no thing'. It is not the nature of the mind to stay with 'no thing'. The mind has to have some image or some appearance or thing, to keep it going. To stay with that 'no thing' for an instant, the idea of fear arises, a fear that I am going to lose my reason. I am going to lose my identity. It is seemingly hard to stay with 'no thing' because the nature of the mind is to think, it is a movement of energy. It is moving back and forth constantly.

To stay with 'no thing' means no energy is going into the thinking, so thinking cannot happen without the energy.

Q: A lot of teachers say that there is no doer-ship and that all is destiny but you say that there is something you can do and that is to stay with the question 'who am I?'.

Yes, but who is the doer? When you talk about destiny, destiny for whom?

Who is it that needs to stick to the question of 'who am I?'

The only instrument that that Pure Intelligence has got is this thinking mind. Intelligence functioning through the mind is nothing but that Pure Intelligence vibrating into a pattern, which we call thought. We attribute these thoughts to a 'me' or a separate entity. They are nothing other than this Pure Intelligence Energy.

Investigate and see that it is so.

Q: So, what would you tell somebody who believed that they were still an individual, believed that they were a personality with a name attached to it—what would you tell them to do?

Well, if someone were to come to me and say that 'I am seeking truth or reality', I would say that what you are seeking you already are! So it is foolish to carry on the search. The only place the search started from is in the mind. It can't start anywhere else and it can't continue anywhere else than in the mind. When I realize or when it is pointed out that it is foolish to carry on the search in the mind, what must happen? If I say to you 'Full stop—the search is over'—what you do? Wouldn't there be a pause? In that pause wouldn't there be a realization that I have not disappeared—I have not fallen apart—I have not disintegrated—I am still here without that thinking mind—then there must be a glimpse of understanding that everything that we seemingly believe relies on that mind. Without that mind the functioning is still happening—you're still breathing, hearing, seeing, thinking, still tasting touching smelling.

Living-ness is still happening without the mind seemingly running the show, which it has done for years. Once that glimpse is there—that there is functioning happening, it is seen as a place of stillness. This is the aim of the meditators, to quieten the mind to that place of stillness. I say that is the wrong way because to quieten the mind, you have to use the mind to quieten the mind and all that is, is conflict in the mind.

It is one thought fighting against another thought. In just the seeing of the fact, that there is no answer in the mind.

It is just like you come up here to look for your watch when you know that you left it in the kitchen. It is foolish to look up here. In the twenty or thirty years that you have been seeking, looking for the answer in the mind, you have never found it.

However you are not an idiot because you have solved a lot of other problems through the mind. But you have not found the answer to life in the mind. Surely there must come a time when you realize that it is futile to look in the mind. Especially when the traditions tell me that the answer is not there.

Q: In terms of the futility of looking in the mind, what you always say is that the false cannot stand up to investigation. So how do we start to investigate?

Come back to the only reality that you are absolutely certain of—the fact of your own Being. Everything else is a mental concept. But you cannot negate your being-ness.

Staying with that being-ness or the thought 'I am', which is the nearest thing you can get to the being-ness with the mind. That is the primary thought.

Stay with that, come back to that.

Q: How do you define staying with the thought 'I am'?

Whenever it moves away to 'I am this' or 'I am that' bring it back to just 'I Am'. Also have an affectionate awareness of just being 'I Am'—be warm towards that 'I am-ness'.

Love that 'I am-ness'—that is the first point where the mind comes into it. You will realize after awhile that you do not have to say 'I am' to know that *you are.* You have known this all the time—you don't go around saying 'I am', 'I am' repeatedly. You are still functioning, the living-ness is still going on, other thoughts are coming in, other activities are taking place but it all comes back to that sense of presence that expresses through the mind as the thought 'I am'. That is the only reality that you cannot negate.

Stay with that long enough—be affectionate towards it—then there is a seeming response to that warmness. That warmness may only be a mental warmness but there will be a seeming response to that warmness and that warmness will well up through your being-ness, through you body and through the mind. It will suffuse that being-ness and bring about the change that is necessary.

Q: So it is as if it is acknowledged.

Exactly—that is a beautiful way to put it. There is a passage in the Bible that says: 'Acknowledge Him in all thy ways and He will direct thy path'. Now most of us interpret that as somebody out there but it means to acknowledge that essence, that intelligence that you are. In acknowledging that, the direction comes through that.

Q: I would like to stay with the subtlety of this 'I am', can you say more about this?

Have a closer look at 'I am'—it is not 'I was' nor is it 'I will be'. It is expressing that presence. It is pure presence. 'I am'. Presence!—not the past—not the future. The actuality is always Now. You do not have to use the term 'I am'.

You see, that primary thought 'I am' is too subtle for the mind to grasp, so it adds to it 'I am this'—'I am that'—'I am the fear'—'I am the anger'—'I am the anxiety, depression or whatever'. Just see that thought as the expression of that presence. Then what must you be—you must be that presence. That is all that there is. It is Omnipresence. These words are presence—that is how they are appearing—they are appearing presently. As you read these words, they are appearing presently. This chair that I am sitting in is presence. You are presence. Everything is presence. It is all That.

We take the appearance, as real rather than in seeing its essence, which is presence.

Q: There is no process of awakening to this understanding, is that right?

Yes, that is right. If it is omnipotence—omniscience and omnipresence—when and who has ever been separate from it? When? Who? and How?—could there be any separation from it? If that idea of separation is seen for what it is—an erroneous belief, a phantom—what process could there be?

You see we have hypnotized ourselves into believing that we are this separate 'I'—this separate entity—this individual. That is not going to die down overnight or immediately.

The seeing of it is immediate but the old habit patterns will come up again and again—because patterns are repetition. Repeating thought patterns of who and what we think we are.

The continuity of thought becomes feeling and emotion. It all has gone on so frequently and for so long and that is why it will not just disappear overnight.

Q: *These sentient beings called humans have been around for tens of thousands of years, are you saying that they are all wrong?*

I know that I was wrong in believing that I was a sentient human being and from that I have the freedom from all those erroneous beliefs. I am not the only one— I have read various books and from that can see that all through the ages there have always been so called people with this understanding. They have carried this message through those tens of thousands of years— right back to the so-called mythical primal guru from the beginning of time.

Q: *You often quote Christ where he said 'I am the light of the world'*

'I am the way—I am the truth—I am the light' not meaning himself—he means come back to that 'I am'.

Q: *That is your interpretation.*

Yes—that is my interpretation.

Q: Who is that 'me' or 'my'?

That is just the terms we use in conversation. I am not afraid to use the words. I use the words just the same as they have always been used. Just the same as I will use the words 'what a beautiful blue sky' knowing full well that the sky is not blue. *(It appears to be blue)*

Knowing full well that there is no center here. *(no 'me').*

It is quite simple—the false cannot stand up to investigation. The mind will make up all sorts of tricks—it will invent a subconscious—a super-conscious and all sorts of different degrees and levels of the mind and seek the answer there. As I say, there have been people all through those thousands of years that say 'come back to where it all begins—that Being-ness'

Q: So in that recognition of inattention when you recognize that you are not just attentive to awareness, there is no guilt. There is freedom, in that recognition—you are.

Exactly!

Q: Although I no longer believe in a process, it still seems that the more time I spend being aware of awareness, that something continually feels like it is opening. It is almost like the perception gets wider, subtler.

Exactly and with that you would find that the thought processes are lessening.

Q: There is an absence of thinking a lot of the time.

135

So, in that absence of thinking, what must you be with? Pure Awareness or pure Consciousness. Then, as the range expands, everything is taken in, less and less is excluded and the perception is wider and wider. The greater the perception of what is—is.

What Is—is Pure Intelligence Energy registering everything just as it is. There is no thinking process in that. The thinking process will alter—modify or correct what is registering. To do that it must refer to a past event—image or experience—which is the 'me'.

So then everything is relative to that 'me'—the self-center. Now if it is not relative to that—if it is just What Is—then what can you say about it and what is wrong with it?

Isn't it functioning and expressing beautifully As Is?

Everything appears on that Pure Presence Awareness. That is just a pure registering and there is no experience in that whatsoever.

Q: So a preference for silence through meditation is missing the point?

How can I prefer the silence to the chatter? What difference do either make when they are appearance only?

Nothing has touched that awareness—that 'I am'. Nothing can contaminate it and nothing can come near it—it is bodiless—mind-less—birth-less—death-less.

Q: How would you describe awareness without using the words 'I am' or 'a sense of presence'?

Pure awareness—pure registering of What Is—your hearing right now—seeing right now—everything is registering just as it is. That doesn't mean to say that is an homogenous blob. Everything is distinguished and registered but it is not named. It is not given a name— it is just as is.

Q: What is it that makes us begin to search for truth?

The seeming search comes from the idea of separation—as soon as that 'I' thought comes up—that 'I' implies separation. Separation is insecurity— vulnerability. There is immediate insecurity with that 'I' thought.

That separation is only a seeming separation—it is only how it appears. Anything in this manifestation can be broken down into pure energy. If this globe called the Earth were to be blown into little pieces— would any of the energy be lost? The Earth is gone but would anything be lost? It would all be out there in space—nothing would be lost.

Q: So the individual is just a bundle of memories that is seemingly separate—however there appears to be immense diversity in the guise of individuals.

Exactly and even in those seeming individuals are in the pairs of opposites—male and female and that attraction brings them together to carry on this diverse appearance. But what has happened really? Nothing! So if you know that nothing has happened are you going to leave the play—just like if you're in a stage production playing the villain—when you know that you are playing a role, as soon as the play is over— you take off the make up, your mask or disguise and go home and have a good sleep. So, when you see that all that is going on is a play of Consciousness then you still take part in the role—as a seeming individual. Knowing the truth about it—that there is no such thing as an 'individual'.

The very idea of an individual implies something as being separate from something else.

This is confronting to many, based on belief. Any belief or non-belief becomes a reference point and everything is judged from that point of view. Then that becomes another self-center or reference point just the same as the 'I' or the 'me'.

So, here in this body-mind there are no set beliefs and there are no set opinions—I can have opinions but they are not set in concrete. Just the same as I can say 'I' or 'me' and that is not set either.

Q: What about the room full of seekers and the guru—even in 'this understanding' there still is something going on, in that there is the guru and a bunch of seekers. Isn't there some way of transcending that?

The way is—for those people that come along—is to immediately see themselves as equal—I can speak this for the rest of my life and there will still be millions that won't see the truth in it. They must test it for themselves.

Q: So many seem to miss this suggestion to look for themselves—to ask the questions of themselves and let the intelligence energy come up within themselves. It took five months for me to actually hear your suggestion and actually try it.

Yes—but the difference with you is that you kept

coming back. It was the same in my case—it went on for years and years until I arrived in the presence of Nisargadatta. By this time, I had to look. By this time, with all the seeking in the mind and all the *kundalini* and spiritual experiences—as I say—you can have many, many spiritual experiences but there is only one spiritual awakening. Those experiences are like the carrot before the donkey. They were leading me on more and more. That can be a trap too, because you can just want the experiences. But seemingly, somewhere along the line, the mind seemed to get fed up with it all and it packed up—then the truth was there ready and waiting as it always had been, to rush into that little gap and take over.

Q: This misconception of enlightenment where there is as if —some place to attain—some place to be.

What is there—or who is there to be enlightened? It is only this 'me' that believes itself to be unenlightened or not whole or not complete. If you look at that and see that this 'me' is only an image—it is an idea—of itself it cannot see, it cannot be aware. It has no power whatsoever. So, how can that thought, which has no power, ever become whole or complete? By its very nature as in the nature of thinking is to divide. All the thinking process is—is division into the pairs of opposites. If its very nature is to divide, then how can it become whole?

You must be able to see that the only time that it can become whole is when there is no thought.

Then the wholeness is there—which was always there.

Q: When we hear this message, quite often we set out on a

quest to have no thought.

Yes, which is wrong again, because it is just a matter of seeing thought and understanding the way that it functions—then it has lost its hold.

You see the 'me' can't change anything. The 'me' is the mind and the mind cannot change the mind.

Q: There are many seekers who are offended by this concept of non-doer-ship. You are not driven to change anything.

Not driven to change anything but if that activity comes up where I am participating in change—then that is what is happening. That is what has been happening for the last 20 years—sitting here seemingly participating in changing seeming individuals and as a seeming person sitting here doing it. Nothing is really happening.

Q: The world is on a self-improvement quest now, what about that?

It is all based again on that seeming self-centre, 'me' and the 'other'. You see, as soon as there is a 'me' which is a reference point, then there must be the 'other'. If there is anger then there is only a 'me' that can be angry.

If there is fear, then it can only be a 'me' that can be fearful. If there is a seeming depression then it can only be a 'me' that can be depressed. That 'me' is based on the past.

If I see clearly that the 'me' is only an idea—an idea or image—it is not the center—it is not solid—there is nothing solid there—that there is no center there, then when these things come up, then they are seen in a new light. So it is a fresh and new experience that is happening right now.

Being identified as a 'me' then as they arise they are named as 'fear' or 'depression' from the past—they are immediately named. But if it is seen and not named then what happens to it?

Q: It begins to fade.

Even if doubt arises about this—if that is seen clearly as another idea—another thought.

Who is doubting? The mind comes up stronger fighting to keep its seeming hold on you.

But if it is looked at in every shape and every form and in every direction, if the falseness of it is constantly seen, then there is no way that it can ever take hold.

The mind is functioning here, now with these words coming out—it has to. The thought is expressed as word. Immediately it comes out—then it is finished. There is no carry on—like 'did I say the right thing'? 'Does that sound correct?' You see there is no reference point that it is constantly referred to.

Q: Who are we to each other?

Consciousness is speaking to Consciousness. How else could it be? Can you conceive of or perceive of anything outside of Consciousness? No, so all this manifestation must be the content of Consciousness. Now, can the content of Consciousness be different than Consciousness? So it is Consciousness speaking to Consciousness—Awareness speaking to Awareness— Intelligence Energy.

Q: *A lot of people give themselves a hard time thinking that they could or should have done it better and that Life has not given them the tools to get through the situations they are in. How does this help them?*

It does not help them at all. It is the same in my own case—years ago I thought the same.

Now I see how beautifully it all fitted in. The pain, the fear, the anger and violence—the resentment and self-pity—the greed, the envy, all these things had their place—or I wouldn't be sitting here today. These things that I carried around with me for years—I am glad they happened but there is no one to be glad either.

You see what I am trying to get at? They happened the way they happened.

Q: *What about thought, how would you explain thought?*

Well, what is a thought—thought is only a movement of energy. It is only energy expressing as a thought—then another thought. The same applies to a belief.

All thoughts come and go—they appear and then disappear. You are prior to thought.

All of the appearance is transient. In the immediacy of this moment everything is registered as it is. It is seen.

There is only One Reality, Thou art That. The world is real but not as it appears.

Q: *A lot of us seem to suffer from what we think life should be like.*

Yes—Life is! The same as What Is. It is not what I think it should be. Life is.

If you look at it closely—Life lives on life. There is no death—life cannot know death.

Q: You would agree that when the body dies the body ceases to function. But that is not death because the energy cannot go anywhere.

The pattern of energy breaks down but life is there in the breaking down process. Another pattern will appear.

Q: When I look into myself I see no thing.

By what light do you see the no thing? What is light? Light is 'knowing'. Light is energy. You are the light! It shines of itself just like the sun. The sun cannot know darkness.

The further out is shines, the further darkness recedes. It cannot know light either because there is nothing to compare it with. It shines of itself and so that knowingness and being-ness shines of itself.

That energy comes up and shines and focuses through the eyes.

Q: The widening of the ability to perceive, that comes with this investigation, leads one to see that there is nothing to fix.

All the energy in the actuality of the moment is with What Is. If the energy is going into the resistance then there is conflict—there is friction. The energy is seemingly fighting with itself. Trying to fix something is resistance and the friction from that dissipates the energy.

That also, is just What Is.

'As you read these words, they are appearing presently. This chair that I am sitting in is presence. Everything is presence. It is all That.'

CR

7

No Thing

Q: *Bob, from everything that has been pointed out here, can you verify the following statement? 'The ever fresh newness of each moment is 'What Is'. This revelation appears to the individualized consciousness as the conceptual obstacles shift and change with this impact of newness. In the case of this being pointed out in words, that which the words point to is revealed and for a moment the Understanding is glimpsed.*

The mind grasps this new input and begins to 'acquire' it. This process constructs a new series of conceptual obstacles. Then another 'revelation' comes and the process is repeated.

Gradually the conceptual obstacles are reduced in number as the impact of the 'ever fresh' opens up. Eventually the mind sees that it can't keep up with ever fresh newness—it gives up and the spontaneous acceptance of 'what is' is lived. Nothing to 'do', nothing to 'change', 'no one' to do or change anything.

What appears is not different from that which sees it.

Well, let's have a look at what has been said.

Remember we talk about Non Duality, One without second, ever fresh presence awareness just this and nothing else—inconceivable, unimaginable and inexpressible, that IS What IS—'newness of each moment'—implies time—time is mind, thoughts—a concept—a concept is not what is—as it is.

'Individualized consciousness?' Has it got any power or any substance for anything to appear on or to?

If 'understanding is glimpsed' who or what glimpses it. Can the mind 'grasp' anything or 'acquire' anything, if mind itself is only words or concepts, without any substance or ability to stand on their own. 'This process'—more time—a new series—more time— 'another revelation'—'and the process is repeated'— time. 'Gradually, eventually, the mind sees'—can the mind see? 'It gives up'—can the mind which has no power give up or accept. Remember we are talking about ordinary awareness—THAT is ever fresh and I mean not new or old but fresh in the fact of not being touched in any way whatsoever by any appearances or reflections that are conceptualized. Just like seeing and hearing. Is seeing itself ever new or is hearing ever new or is it the content, the translation that is split into the seer and the seen—that gives it the appearance of newness. Seeing is the fact, the actual, the real, the seer and the seen are conceptual, yet seeing is quite ordinary and ever present not needing to be started or stopped in fact it cannot be started or stopped, have a look at your own awareness and see if it is like this or not.

If so what needs to be done and by whom?

What appears is not different from that which sees it, exactly as what appears and that which sees it is mind concepts, a seeming division in the seeing—there is only the seeing, quite ordinary—in its completeness, right now presently, nothing gradual, nothing new, nothing accepted, nothing rejected—just seeing, seeing, seeing.

YOU ARE THAT.

The following is from an Interview with Bob after the compilation of this book.

Bob, what can the reader find in this book?

Following the book, if they have a look at themselves they will see that they are not what they believed themselves to be in the first place. That will bring them to the understanding or the knowing that they are not that separate entity which is the cause of all their problems. If the cause is seen to be false, then what effect can there be. So the so called psychological suffering that humans go through will drop away.

It is not necessary.

Q: In this Understanding when it opens up, what happens to all the memories and expectations of the future?

Memories are still there and can be brought into the moment.

Memory is a good thing when it is utilized. All the beliefs of the separate entity fall away and you realize that things have happened the way they have happened—not because of any personal doership. With regard to the expectations of the future—there is no concern about that. Why be concerned with something that hasn't happened, when you can be with the actuality—the livingness is right now. All the vitality is in that, why waste time with something that hasn't happened when you can be with What Is—totally.

When the conditioning comes upon us we seeming lose sight of our true nature. But when it is pointed to, it is seen again and it is no longer ignored and your back, even though you have never left.

The true nature is no thing but it is the unlimited potential in which all things appear and disappear.

Q: Bob, you have found various writings from different traditions that resonate with this understanding, can you say anything about those writings?

Well, the first one that sort of opened me up was the Advahut Gita, when I was in the Ashram. I knew there was something in that but couldn't quite grasp it. I used to love going back to it and reading it.

Then after Nisargadatta, it was very clear. From then on the things that I read only confirmed it. They might be saying the same thing in different words and in a different way—all they did was confirm what I already knew.

Q: What were some of the other writings you found?

A lot of the Dzogchen scriptures and other ancient scriptures including Sengtsan from the Zen tradition.

Some of these scriptures are put so beautifully and they point to this constantly. They are just flowing from the source, you can see it.

Another scripture says 'be thought free' A lot are mistaken about this as well, they think they have to throw 'this thought' out and the next one out—not thinking that, let the thought be free—let it do what it

148

likes. Just like the clouds are not attached to the sky—they move on.

Q: When I see that the mind is never satisfied and relentlessly tries to capture the knowledge of the present and wants to store it away and go onto search for something else, imagining that it now has it, I see that it is completely useless.

All I need to be is this immediacy.

Well you can't be anything else!

But we don't realize it—you see it is Omnipresence.

So it can't be anything else that That.

Look at those memories from childhood. How do you know those moments? Did you have the same body as you do know? Did you have the same image that you have about yourself now? No. You know it because it is that innate intelligence and that hasn't changed.

That is the definition of reality—'That which never changes'. The body has changed and the image of yourself has changed and the reference point or self centre has changed—but that hasn't.

The whole manifestation is constantly changing.

Everything is That—appearing as different.

That is difficult for the mind to get a hold on.

The mind is time and That has no time. It is beginning-less and endless. 'It' has no space and the mind is space also.

'It' has no dimension. So the mind can never grasp it. The so called 'a moment ago' has not left this Omnipresence. Though it appears to have left.

We give that appearance some distance—I can say 'a moment ago or a year ago' but what are you doing?

You only have to have a concept of a moment ago

and then have a concept of a year ago— then try to have a mental concept of a thousand years ago and what is the difference?

You are the movement... without a reference point where can you say it starts from?

Everything you see is objective, everything you think is an object. You're aware of thinking—so it is an object. But we don't include this body-mind as an object. We think we are that 'seeing objects'—We think we are the subject.

But when I see you—I am seeing an object. So you are just an object also.

When you realize that of yourself— 'I am only an objective also'—there is just seeing then. This is because we can't separate the seeing.

When you look out anywhere you see 'no thing'. Yet it is seen.

What can you call it—that which is seen— if you don't label it. You can't call it anything—so it is 'no thing', so what you are actually seeing is no thing.

Look at it this way—try and show me space. You can't—but you are seeing it!

We are not registering it as a 'thing'. There is no time that you are not seeing it.

Know that you are never distracted—you are never away from that.

You can't seemingly forget it—because when you are seemingly forgetting it—that is it also.

Q: 'Bob, what is the bottom line?'

The bottom line is—

RIGHT HERE — RIGHT NOW

YOU ARE PRESENT
and
YOU ARE AWARE OF BEING PRESENT.

**REALISE THAT YOU
ARE THAT ONE WITHOUT A
SECOND, PURE
PRESENCE AWARENESS
AND
BE WHAT YOU ARE.**

'Pure awareness—pure registering of What Is—your hearing right now-seeing right now—everything is registering just as it is'.

&

Testimonials

'Reading this book will question and challenge what you believe to be reality, what you believe to be the truth. You will begin to see life from an entirely different perspective, one that will free you from the baggage that prevents you from living a happy and fulfilled life. You will understand that there is no one who lives a life but that there is only Life. May this understanding come to you as it did to me through Bob's teaching'.

—David Black

'I first met Bob Adamson two years ago. What first attracted me to his teachings was the One without a second concept of God—Omnipotence, Omniscience and Omnipresence. If God is everything—what room is there for this idea of a self important 'entity' called 'me'. Then came the understanding, that I am not my thoughts—that 'my' life is being lived. And that 'events' are not controlled by 'my' thoughts. Thoughts themselves are an expression of this One Consciousness—or 'Being-ness'. Another realization came, that there is no other 'time' than 'right now'. All power and knowledge are available only in this moment of all presence. The mind itself is but a tool which can only think in terms of a past or a future: it is not the controlling factor.

Bob, who has been very generous with his wisdom, has helped me to see that no matter what is going on in the appearance of life—all is fundamentally 'all right'—from the position of 'right now'. Looking at life from the position of Awareness or Consciousness

—rather than from the shifting reference point of 'me' or 'my' mind has helped in making life more carefree, effortless and productive. I can now see life as a great adventure—an adventure that is happening always Now.

—*Cliff*

What I like in the talking and listening with Bob is his absolute unshakable clarity. When I first listened to Bob, I was full of anger, unhappiness and suffering. That dropped away with the realization as Bob pointed out that I am awareness. He showed me that it was my mind, running over old patterns of torment and creating the suffering. If we are all pure awareness—then 'all' means 'all'—no exceptions—not a 'me' and 'awareness'—but one awareness.

When Bob asked me to look for myself, I saw that there is 'no thing' I can locate called 'me'. There is a collection of ideas and interpretations which I have called 'me'—held in memory—but in truth there is only awareness.

If awareness is all, how can there be a 'me' or any 'other'. We are all that one awareness. Within this understanding—how can there be animosity for any perceived 'other'? If I know that there is just this awareness and nothing else, then how was there ever any separation?

Bob expresses the truth with such clarity and simplicity that there is no misunderstanding and no doubt. No need to understand jargon or interpret what he says—it is clear. There is nothing to 'do'—no 'practice' to pursue—I understand that I am awareness—now.

—*Jan Dobbs*

The search started in childhood. I first looked at Christianity and then moved to science and logic to give the answers in life. As an adult, my search moved to psychology and later to eastern philosophy and Buddhism—but I was getting closer! By my early 50's, I was hot on the trail! It was the Non-Dual writings of 20th Century Sages. I even traveled overseas to meet some of them.

Then in '94, I met Bob. His approach was very different and very simple. 'The answer does not lie in the mind' he said to me. At other times, he would ask …'and who is it who is asking the question'?

I now smile at how furious I felt at these times. Well, after a while at Bob's meetings, it became very clear that there is nothing to get and no one to get it. I am not that searcher and (*paradoxically*) never was.

Please read this book. The profound wisdom in Bob's spoken words are simple and beautifully clear. They show you that your search is futile; they show you what you are not—they show you what you are and what you have always been. And at that—you may laugh and laugh!

—*Col*

Bob clearly and simply points back to what I am.

Realizing my true nature has changed my life.

—*Brione*

Meeting Bob Adamson or reading his comments on life is nothing short of a gift.

Simply and humbly, yet in no uncertain terms, he makes it perfectly clear 'Who you already are', by relentlessly pointing out 'Who and what you are not'.

Bob's message is not polluted by spiritual carrots

and conceits. He has no need to slowly impart to you the imaginary 'something' that the mind likes to envision it might 'one day' *(in the future)* attain. Instead, he points with supreme conviction to the only thing or 'no thing' that cannot be negated—which is our own 'present awareness'—'This and nothing but this—Unaltered—Unmodified and Uncorrected' I highly recommend reading and 'listening' to Bob Adamson. With great love and appreciation for this man.

Contact:

Bob Adamson

4/950 Burke Road

Deepdene, Melbourne

Australia 3103

Tel: 03 9817 5878 or 03 9817 1949

Email: adamson7@austarmetro.com.au
or
http://members.austarmetro.com.au/~adamson7

*Meetings are held on Tuesdays and
Thursdays at 7.30 pm
&
Sundays at 5.00 pm*

Or Contact:

Gilbert Schultz at
tigereyez@bigpond.com

Contact:

Bob Adamson
4/950 Bruke Road,
Deepdene, Melbourne,
Australia, Zip 3103
Tel.: 03 9817 58
eMail: adamson7@austarmetro.com

Meetings are held on Tuesdays and Thursdays at 7.30 pm
&
Sundays at 5.00 pm

Contact:

Clive Smithson
beeryweb@bigpond.com